Paul N. (Paul Nooncree) Hasluck

House Decoration

Comprising Whitewashing, Paperhanging, Painting, etc.

Paul N. (Paul Nooncree) Hasluck

House Decoration
Comprising Whitewashing, Paperhanging, Painting, etc.

ISBN/EAN: 9783337119300

Printed in Europe, USA, Canada, Australia, Japan

Cover: Foto ©Lupo / pixelio.de

More available books at **www.hansebooks.com**

HOUSE DECORATION

COMPRISING

WHITEWASHING, PAPERHANGING, PAINTING, ETC.

WITH NUMEROUS ENGRAVINGS AND DIAGRAMS

EDITED BY

PAUL N. HASLUCK

EDITOR OF "WORK" NEW SERIES, AUTHOR OF "HANDYBOOKS FOR
HANDICRAFTS," ETC. ETC.

CASSELL AND COMPANY, Limited
LONDON, PARIS & MELBOURNE
1897

ALL RIGHTS RESERVED

PREFACE.

THIS Handbook contains, in a form convenient for everyday use, a comprehensive digest of the knowledge of House Decoration scattered over ten thousand columns of WORK, the weekly journal it is my fortune to edit—and supplies concise information on the general principles of the craft on which it treats.

In preparing for publication in book form the mass of relevant matter contained in the volumes of WORK, much that was tautological in character had to be rejected. The remainder necessarily had to be arranged anew, altered and largely re-written. From these causes the contributions of many are so blended that the writings of individuals cannot be distinguished for acknowledgment. However, it may be mentioned that a series of articles from the pen of a well-known London decorator are incorporated in the text.

Readers who may desire additional information respecting special details of the matters dealt with in this Handbook, or instruction on kindred subjects, should address a question to WORK so that it may be answered in the columns of that journal.

P. N. HASLUCK.

La Belle Sauvage, London.

CONTENTS.

CHAP.		PAGE
I.—On Colour and Paints		9
II.—Pigments		29
III.—Oils, Driers, Varnishes, etc.		47
IV.—Tools used by Painters		59
V.—How to Mix Oil Paints		74
VI.—Distemper or Tempera Painting		91
VII.—Whitewashing and Decorating a Ceiling		103
VIII.—Painting a Room		114
IX.—Papering a Room		133
X.—Embellishment of Walls and Ceilings		144

LIST OF ILLUSTRATIONS.

FIG.		PAGE
1.—The Mixing of Colours	. . . . .	15
2.—Primary Colours Applied to Form on Owen Jones's Principle	. . . .	16
3.—Positions of Primary Colours Reversed	. . .	17
4.—Cornice Tinting suited for a Bedroom	. . .	18
5.—Cornice Tinting suited for a Sitting-room	. .	19
6.—Cornice Tinting suited for a Dining-room	. .	20
7.—Cornice Tinting suited for a Drawing-room	. .	21
8.—Ceiling and Dado Colourings	. . . .	23
9.—Cornice Colourings, after Owen Jones	. .	24
10.—Ordinary House-Painter's Brush	. . .	60
11.—House-Painter's ordinary Oval Brush	. .	61
12.—Cheap Style of Brush, with Copper Binding	.	61
13.—English Sash Tool	. . . . . .	61
14.—Small Sash Tool	. . . .	61
15.—German Paint Tool	. . . . . .	61
16.—Long-Haired Sash Tool	. . . . .	62
17.—Quilled Sash Tool	. . . . . .	62
18.—Sash Tool for General Use	. . . .	62
19.—Sash-Painting Tool	. . . . . .	62
20.—Hog-hair Fitch in round Tin	. . . .	62
21.—Hog-hair in flat Tin	. . . . . .	62
22.—Hog-hair flat Tool	. . . . . .	62
23.—French round Tool	. . . . . .	63
24.—Oval bevelled Varnish Brush	. . . .	63
25.—Flat Varnish Brush in Tin	. . . .	63
26.—Varnishing Fitch	. . . . . .	63
27.—House-Painters' Dusting Brush	. . .	64
28.—Stencil Tool	. . . .	64
29.—Lining Fitch in flat Handle	. . . .	64
30.—Hog-hair Lining Fitch	. . . . .	64
31.—Section of Straight-Edge	. . . . .	65
32.—Best form of Distemper Brush	. . . .	65
33.—Washing Brush	. . . . . .	65
34.—Paddle Distemper Brush on Nailed Stock	.	65
35.—Limer, used with a long Handle	. . .	66
36.—Scotch Distemper Brush	. . . . .	66
37.—Pasting Brush	. . . .	66

FIG.		PAGE
38.—Stippler		67
39.—Stippler with Reversible Handle		67
40.—Stippler with Bridge Handle		67
41 to 44.—How to Tie a Paint Brush		68
45.—Preserving Paint Brushes		69
46.—Paint Straining Sieve		70
47.—Patent Paint Strainer		70
48.—Chisel-pointed Stopping Knife		71
49.—Stopping Knife		71
50.—Chisel or Broad Knife		71
51.—Palette Knife		72
52.—Glazier's Putty Knife		72
53.—Glazier's Hacking Knife		72
54.—Portable Balcony in Position for Use		73
55.—Perspective Sketch of Portable Balcony		73
56.—Ceiling divided into four Simple Panels		110
57.—Ceiling with Circular Centre		111
58.—Ceiling with Octagonal Centre		112
59.—Ceiling with Square Central Panel		113
60.—Paperhanger's Brush		137
61.—Paperhanger's Roller		137
62.—Four Designs for Ashlar Work Dado		144
63.—Coloured Plaster Cornice with Stencilled Frieze		145
64.—Grecian Style Pattern for Stencil		146
65.—Design for Stencil Frieze		147
66.—Design for Base Border		147
67.—Stencil Designs for entire Wall		148
68.—Design for Filling enlarged		149
69.—Design for Dado enlarged		149
70.—Border Ornament for Ceiling		150
71.—Deep Frieze Ornament		150
72.—Base Border Ornament		151
73.—Design for Border		152
74.—Design for Border		152
75.—Deep Frieze Decoration		153
76.—Dado in Borders and Panels		153
77.—Corner of Ceiling Stencilled in Colours		154
78.—How to Draw a Stencil		155
79.—Design for Ceiling Embellishment		156

HOUSE DECORATION.

CHAPTER I.

ON COLOUR AND PAINTS.

THE work of the house-painter chiefly consists in applying an impervious coat, of which linseed-oil is the base, to the exposed surfaces of buildings, either as a preventive against decay or for ornamental purposes, or both. In external work, the chief uses of paint are to protect the material beneath from the destructive influence of alternate wet and dry, from frost, the sun's rays, and the acids present in the atmosphere, especially in that of large towns, and to write names over shop fronts, called facia-writing. In internal work, paint is principally employed for decorative and ornamental purposes; and it is to these that this book is devoted.

It is necessary that the student and worker in paints should clearly understand the difference between the two terms *pigments* and *colour*, oftentimes confounded. Colour is but a *sensation* conveyed to the brain by the action of light upon the nerve-fibres of the retina. Pigments, on the other hand, are substances which, when acted upon by light, absorb certain of the rays of colour therein contained, and, by either reflection or transmission, give forth that particular colour by which they are known. It will readily be understood that colour and pigment is not in any way a distinction of terms only.

The house-painter, however, deals with pigments, colour being the resultant effect. The term pigment, as already mentioned, implies the substances or materials that are laid upon surfaces to impart colour, and the laws that govern the mixing of pigments are not identical with those that control the blending of colours. For instance, the addition of yellow pigment to blue will result in a mixture having a green hue; although the union of blue and yellow colours will result in white.

It will be well at the commencement of this handbook to briefly state the meaning of the more technical terms used in the text, so that the author's meaning may be made plain to the reader's understanding.

Pigment is any colouring substance or material from which a dye, a paint, or the like, may be prepared; the term is applied particularly to the refined and purified colouring matter ready for mixing with an appropriate vehicle.

Oil-colour is a paint made by grinding a colouring substance in oil; the term is applied to such paints taken in a general sense.

Vehicle is any liquid with which a pigment is applied, including whatever gum, wax, or glutinous or adhesive substance is combined with it. Water is used in fresco and in water-colour painting, the colours being consolidated with gum-arabic; size is used in distemper painting. In oil painting, the fixed oils of linseed, nut, and poppy are used; in encaustic, wax is the vehicle.

Driers is drying oil, a substance being mingled with the oil used in oil painting to make it dry quickly.

Oil of turpentine, or spirit of turpentine, is a colourless oily hydrocarbon of a pleasant aromatic odour, obtained by the distillation of crude turpentine, which is an exudation of the terebinth, or turpentine-tree.

Varnish is a viscid liquid, consisting of a solution of resinous matter in an oil or a volatile liquid, laid on work with a brush or otherwise. When applied, the varnish soon dries, either by evaporation or by chemical action, and the resinous part forms thus a smooth hard surface with a beautiful gloss, capable of resisting to a greater or less degree the influence of air and moisture. According to the sorts of solvents employed, the ordinary kinds of varnish are divided into three classes— spirit, turpentine, and oil varnishes.

Tempera is a mode or process of painting: the term is applied especially to early Italian painting, common vehicles of which were yolk of egg, yolk and white of egg mixed together, the white juice of the fig-tree, and the like. Distemper is a preparation of opaque or body colour, in which the pigments are tempered or diluted with weak glue or size (if tempera) instead of oil, usually for scene-painting or for walls and ceilings of rooms.

It may be well here to further define some of the terms that are frequently used in treating of colour. The principal quality of a colour is its *hue*. It is this that first appeals to the sight, and by which we are able to name the colour; and we speak of it as red of an orange hue, or green of a bluish hue.

Pure colour is absolutely free from any admixture of white. Brightness, or *luminosity*, is a term that has reference to the amount of light the colour reflects to the eye. These three qualities—hue, purity, and brightness, or luminosity—are termed the constants of colour.

The term *tone* must not be confounded with brightness. The latter has reference to the quantity of sensation caused to the optic nerves by a given area, and is measured by the amount of light reflected by the colour.

Tones are estimated by the absolute amount of colour sensation they excite. They may be grouped into three series for every possible hue or kind of colour, according as these hues are admixed with white, with black, or with both black and white, or grey. Apart from any alteration of hue which may occur by such admixtures, it may be affirmed that a normal colour is weakened or reduced by the addition of white, producing tones in a scale of series from deep to pale; and a normal colour is made darker, but not deeper, by the addition of black.

Tones belonging to any of the above series are commonly spoken of as shades, but it is better to limit the use of this term to admixtures with black. A scale is a regular series of such tones as those which have been defined above. So each hue admits of three scales:—

(1) The reduced scale—that is, the normal hue mixed with progressive increments of white, thus forming tints.

(2) The darkened scale—that is, the normal hue mixed with progressive increments of black, thus forming shades.

(3) The dulled scale—that is, the normal hue mixed with progressive increments of grey, thus forming broken tints, commonly called "greys."

There are several ways of preparing a series of tones belonging to each of the scales, assuming that we are dealing with pure pigments, and not with coloured lights. To obtain a scale of, say, ten tints of a colour, add one-twentieth of zinc-white for the first tint, two-twentieths for the second, three-twentieths for the third, and so on up to half and half for the tenth tint.

In a lecture on "Colour," given in February, 1894, at the Royal Institution, by Professor Shelford Bidwell, amongst the curious things the audience learned was the fact that green is not, as generally supposed, a compound colour, made up of blue and yellow. This was clearly demonstrated by projecting a disc of pure blue upon a screen, and over it another disc of pure yellow. The result was not green, but white. The explanation of the popular error is that when ordinary impure blues and yellows are mixed, the dominant colours neutralise each other, and leave the impurities visible. These impurities invariably show up as greens. Yellow itself was proved by lantern-slide to be capable of being made by green and red rays projected jointly on the screen.

Lord Rayleigh also lectured on "Colour" at the Royal Institution during the same month, and, in dealing with the colours of opaque objects, showed that the usual statement that such colours are due to the reflection of light requires qualifying. Besides reflection, there is absorption. A glass dishful of coloured transparent liquid appears black until some object which reflects light is placed behind it; and practically the same thing takes place with coloured paper or cloth. Water and clear glass reflect scarcely any rays, whilst snow or powdered glass reflects nearly all. The irregularly disposed surfaces of the crystals throw off light in every direction; but as soon as a fluid medium having the same reflecting index is used to fill up the interstices, transparency is restored. A vessel filled with powdered glass and cold bisulphide of carbon allows only green rays to pass through, but on being warmed, only yellow rays appear.

To illustrate the effect of mixing white with colour, a disc was made to rotate quickly, and segments of varying proportions fixed to it, one after another, produced variations in tint—the ruddiest crimson appearing as pale pink when a large proportion of the colour was covered by the white. By using a non-reflecting black in place of the white, the hue was changed to a darker one. Newton essayed to work out the resultant of a number of colours when mixed, just as the resultant of a number of forces can be ascertained by mathematics; but the method he adopted is now proved to have been inaccurate. The lecturer reminded his audience that blue, green, and red are now considered as the primary colours, yellow having been rejected from scientific inclusion. Pure green and pure red rays projected from a lantern on a white screen produce yellow.

Recent researches on the phenomena of colours render it likely that every tint, and hue, and shade of dye will ere long be accurately describable in words alone. Lord Rayleigh pointed out as an instance of colour compounds that 100 parts of blue, 50 of white, and 42 of red produce the same colour as 64 parts yellow and 128 blue. Again, 135 parts of black, 21 of white, and 36 of yellow compound a colour identical with 123 of red and 67 of green. Thus is colour reducible to formulas not unlike chemical equations.

For the purpose of practical illustration, let us assume that the early chromatic equivalents of M. Chevreul and George Field are correct—viz., that the primary, or first, colours are pure red, pure blue, and pure yellow; that each primary is contrasted harmoniously with or neutralised by a mixture of the two other primaries in certain proportions, which mixture is named a secondary; and, further, that each secondary is balanced by a certain mixture of the two remaining secondaries, termed a *tertiary* colour. The total purport of this is, therefore: primaries—red, blue, and yellow; secondaries—purple (red and blue), green (blue and yellow) and orange (yellow and red); tertiaries—olive (green and purple), russet (orange and purple), and citrine (orange and green).

The primary pigments, being the first simple division, consist of blues, reds, and yellows. By combining chemically suitable blue and red, we obtain purple; with red and yellow we get orange; whilst blue and yellow pigments combine to give us green colours or sensations. These resultant admixtures of any two primaries are termed *secondary* colours; and again by a similar process of mixing, in certain proportions, two of the secondary pigments together, we obtain the third distinct class into which we divide our colours, which third division is known as the *tertiary* colours.

With the primary pigments at hand, almost every variety of colour requisite or desirable for our ordinary use can be prepared.

The diagram on p. 15 shows the complementary colour to each primary, and the two complementaries to each secondary:

        Primaries: Red, Blue, Yellow.
        Secondaries: Purple, Orange, Green.
        Tertiaries: Brown, Slate, Olive.

A primary colour is complementary to the colour formed by mixture of the other two primaries:

        Red complementary to Green.
        Blue complementary to Orange.
        Yellow complementary to Purple.

A secondary is complementary to the colour formed

by mixture of the other two secondaries, and also to the primary to which it is complementary:

Green complementary to Brown or Red.
Orange complementary to Slate or Blue.
Purple complementary to Olive or Yellow.

A colour's pure complement is formed of equal parts of each, and in this diagram all colours are as above—though, of course, different tones can be made up by unequal proportions. Light being the source of colour, it can only be divided into its components.

The dominant impressions that the primary colours

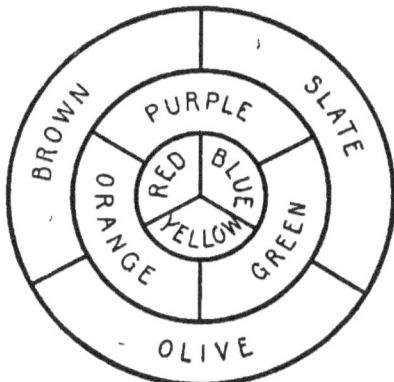

Fig. 1.—The Mixing of Colours.

convey to the mind through the vision are briefly as follows. Red gives richness and warmth of sentiment, and appears stationary of position when applied to form. Blue speaks of space and coolness, and will give a retiring effect to form. Yellow conveys several sensations, and is most difficult to successfully manipulate: it is considered chiefly an exciting power, which may verge from high brilliancy and lustre to very garish and irritating effects. Beyond this, in its application to form, yellow has a prominent or advancing appearance.

Every definite colour has its contrast and complementary: that is, a colour in appearance and sentiment directly opposite, but which, when placed in juxtaposition, improves and heightens the effect, and combines so as to produce the sensation of *colour harmony.* In the selection of colour for decoration, *contrast* is therefore one scheme we may choose.

With various sentiments of colour under one roof, satisfactory contrast should exist between them.

The alternative scheme for colouring is harmony,

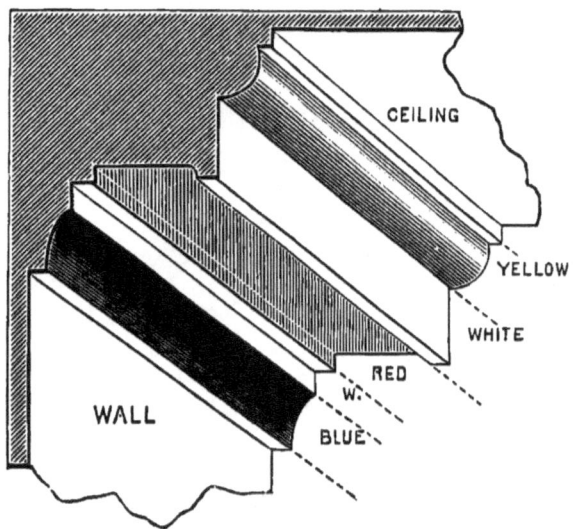

Fig. 2.—Primary Colours Applied to Form on Owen Jones's Principle.

which is produced by employing a graduated scale of colour.

Owen Jones gave in the year 1852 this dogma or proposition:—Colour is used to assist in the development of form, and to distinguish objects, or parts of objects, one from another. Mr. Ruskin's theory is—that the first great principle of architectural colour is this: let it be visibly independent of form.

Since these theories were propounded, much progress has been made in decorative art and colouring and modern conclusions concerning the relationship of colour to form now incline to this :—That the two systems, whilst being quite distinctive and separate, may be so combined as to materially enhance the beauty and effect of both.

Here let us turn to Fig. 2, representing the section of a cornice used by Owen Jones to explain his theory. In the shade, red is placed to soften its brightness; on the most prominent form, yellow is put to assist its shape; the concave moulding is coloured blue. White

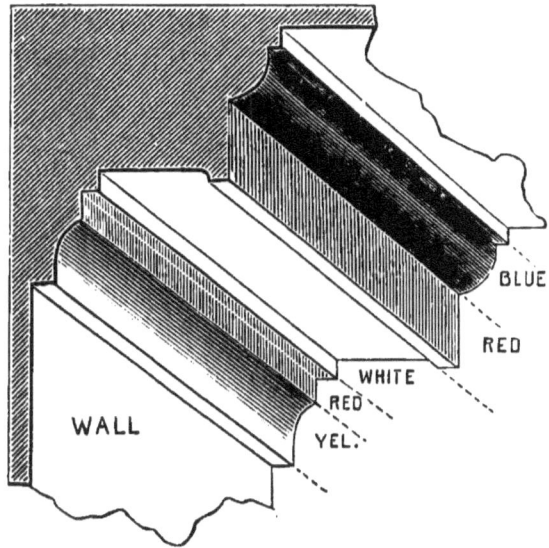

Fig. 3.—Positions of Primary Colours reversed from those shown on p. 16.

intervenes between them on the vertical planes, to prevent one primary impinging on the other. This is really but applying to mouldings the colours best adapted to displaying their shape; it does not secure colour harmony even in the cornice itself, and much less in the cornice and the supporting wall. An idea of how far colour does assist form may be got from Fig. 3, where colour is represented by shade. The scheme of Fig. 2 is as described above; at Fig. 3 the colours are reversed. Colour harmony is still independent of either arrangement.

In sleeping apartments, pure and simple, white must stand pre-eminent as correct expression. Nevertheless, many probably prefer the dominant white toned down with a little warmth (red), or soft repose (blue); or, if badly served with Nature's brilliance and strength, we may use a blithe yellow.

The tinting of an ordinary bedroom cornice is represented in Fig. 4; it assumes a bedroom of cold aspect, with

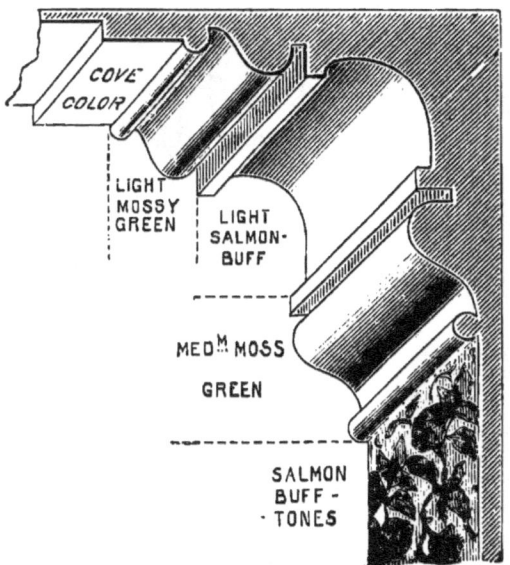

Fig. 4.—Cornice Tinting suited for a Bedroom.

the walls hung with a paper in self-tones of salmon-buff, the flat ceiling being distempered a warm cream, made by mixing raw sienna with white. The mouldings next to the paper should be made a warm mossy green, made from ochre, umber, a little ultramarine green (a blue of very green hue) and a little white. The green hue must be very subdued, since the warm walls will bring it out into prominence. A light tint of warm colour is put in the cove, which, by reason of the shade, will look a little deeper; this same tint is used on the flat, next cornice. The mouldings between cove and flat are coloured a little lighter tint of the moss green, made by adding to the latter some of the ceiling cream-colour. If handled with care and judgment, the result will be harmonious and effective, with only three tints of colour.

Another example (Fig. 5) shows a room cornice which

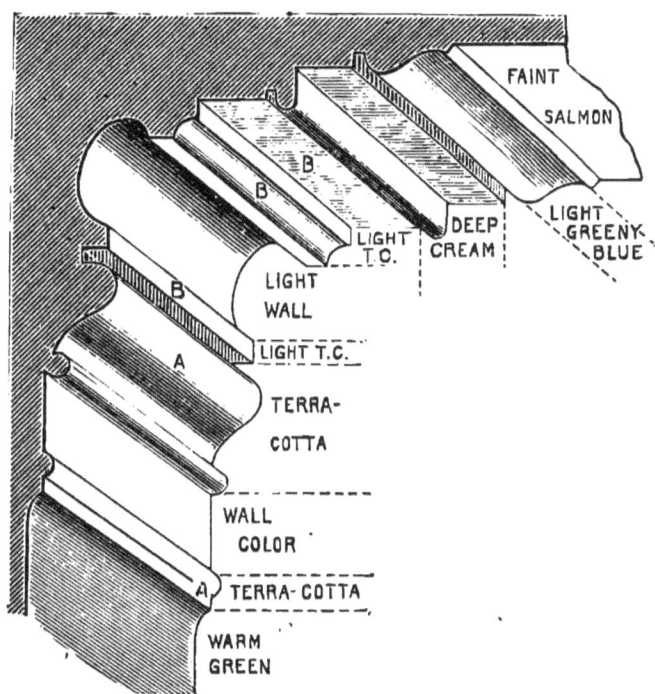

Fig. 5.—Cornice Tinting suited for a Sitting-room.

provides for a neutral, or warm green, flatted wall-colour. Next to this is a soft terra-cotta, or reddish-brown, a few shades darker than the wall; above this a band of wall-colour, and this framed by the previous terra-cotta at A below and a lighter shade at B above. The cove is painted in a lighter and more yellow tint of the walls, bounded also on top by the lighter terra-cotta tint. A deep-cream flat comes next, then the ogee in a light tint of greeny-blue, which is separated from a faint and soft salmon-tint on ceiling by a small cream flat.

Fig. 6 represents colour applied to a cornice in a room over a rich and glowing wall-paper of semi-natural floral

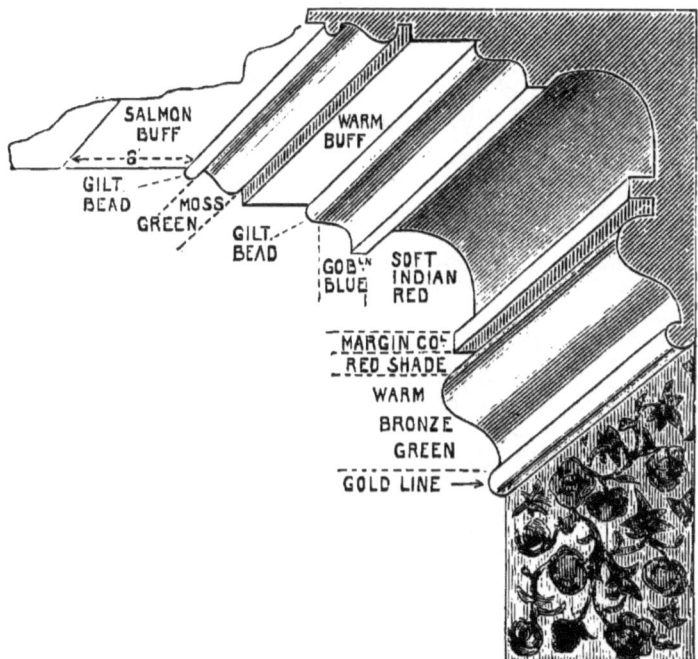

Fig. 6.—Cornice Tinting suited for a Dining-room.

design, the colours being warm greens and browns, with flowers in mixtures of soft rich red, old gold, and a little "gobelin" or greenish-blue. The ceiling is coated with a soft but decided pink tint, made with Venetian red and ochre, and next to cornice there is a margin 8 in. wide in a deeper shade of the same colour. The base of cornice is a medium bronze-green, the cove Indian red and a little white—deeper than the base in tone. The margin colour is put on the flat above a medium tint of soft gobelin blue at the flat and hollow next to the cove, and the remaining members warm buff and a greenish-yellow or light mossy green. The lines and ornament may be in terra-cotta, moss green, and light gobelin blue upon the light pinky-buff of ceiling. In this illustration the place for a little gilding is indicated.

What should be the colour expression of the present

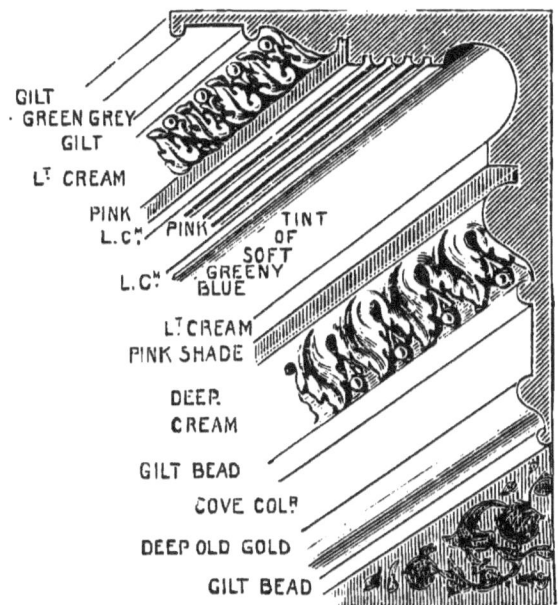

Fig. 7.—Cornice Tinting suited for a Drawing-room.

day drawing-room? White ought to predominate, either in mass or in combination, as tints with other colours. These colours should be yellow to add richness and brilliancy, blue to relieve and enhance it—just as the "field" of blue sky contrasts to the sun. It may be asked, But why not pink or green sentiments? For these general reasons—that light, not heat, should predominate, that light and heat together are inconsistent with the sentiment of such a room, and, further, that true green is not only bilious of temper but almost fatal to mixed combinations.

Fig. 7 is a treatment for the cornice of room having a straw-coloured ceiling and old gold walls; the cornice is coloured in self-tones, or monotones of the same colours. The blue cove tint, though appearing blue against a faint yellow and cream, is, when viewed alone, quite a green tint. The very faint pink-red colour is a tint of Indian red. The creams are made with chromes and umber, and must be clearly compounded to be pleasing.

Next consider the dining-room. Its modern purposes are chiefly displayed by artificial interior light, hence white plays but a humble part in its treatment. Red tones for comfort and warmth are most natural. Red also, although classed as a stationary colour, is safer in practice when toned down with black, or in positions naturally shaded. Try a mass of fiery red, then add an equal proportion of black, and note the resulting sentiment: " prudent heat"—red, shaded with black. Again, add white to red: result—heat still powerfully dominant. A dining-room may be coloured red, of any intensity, with the hall, or room approach, coloured intense green-blue. The result will then be that the red appears more intense and brilliant after looking at the hall colour. Harsh or strong contrast is a matter irrespective of harmony. In an age of temperance and moderation, let colour contrasts be consistent, simple, temperate, and expressive; not overbearing in sentiment, like the ancient Egyptian and Chinese colourings, and sensuous, like the Pompeian.

Halls and staircases are not presented to the eye for long periods, hence their colour expression may not be so arbitrarily stated. If well lighted, we must restrain our hand in the positive sentiments generally; but if badly lighted, then aim to give expression to brilliancy and cheerfulness. When dull and cheerless weather predominates, the warm and cheerful tones are most successful.

The **study** and **library** are open to much divergence

of colour treatment. Either of the positive colour sensations are in keeping with the use of these rooms; but expediency must be studied, and white and yellow are "bad," unless the natural light is very poor.

A pleasing colour and treatment for painting walls is a light green-grey "filling" or upper portion, and a terra-

Fig. 8.—Ceiling and Dado Colourings.

cotta or Indian red colour for the dado or lower portion. This will harmonise admirably with light oak woodwork. "Cream" for the filling would not wear so well, showing discoloration sooner than the above. "Light salmon" would be better, but not so cheerful and harmonious in effect.

The cornice *in its entirety* should in all cases form a frame to the ceiling, the darkest colour to be at the base and the tones to lighten towards the ceiling; but the deepest tones should be darker than the general wall-colour. Fig. 8 shows a scheme for colouring.

Do not fritter time away in putting twenty colours and shades into one cornice; the eye cannot appreciate it, and the effect is lost. To ordinary view, it destroys the breadth of the cornice. Gilding is properly put only on advanced portions, and should always be finished off with a coating of clear size.

A few lines to form the foundation for practice are

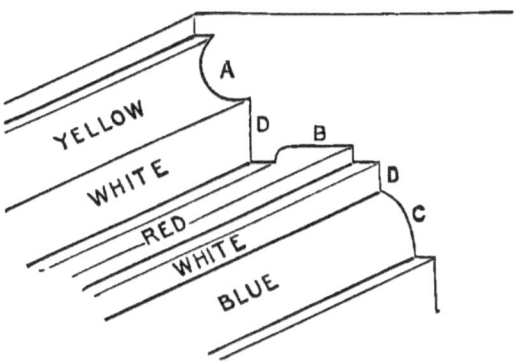

Fig. 9.—Cornice Colourings, after Owen Jones.

here quoted from the late Owen Jones:—"It is evident that (in Fig. 9) as the object must be to cause A to advance, it is here we must put the yellow, both from its position and from its form. On the contrary, we place blue at C as the retiring colour, and assisting the concavity of the moulding. Red, the most positive of all colours, looks best in shadow—we, therefore, place it at B. The fillets or vertical planes at D we make white, as useful in separating the colours from harsh contrast. The positions of the colours are subject to modification, according to circumstance. Red never looks well when seen in a strong light: it is too positive and painful to the eye; on the contrary, in soffits, in hollows, or depths of any kind, it looks most brilliant. Beyond this, use a faint tint instead of white for all but simple bedroom ceiling flats.

Avoid pure or bright colours, especially when they contrast, like blue and yellow, red and green. Mix the tints to a colour similar to the wall paper, then place them somewhat as shown. Avoid much contrast of tone, but give depth." The illustration on page 16 should also be examined in connection with this illustration.

In painting a billiard-room particularly, the range of suitable colour is governed entirely, and limited considerably, by the vivid green mass of cloth covering the billiard-table and the accompanying green shades to the usual gas-lighting arrangement. The selection of colours must not clash with, or in the least detract from, the appearance of the billiard-table. The dominant colour-tone of a room is usually furnished by the walls, and being here the principal surface the eye will rest upon after leaving the green table, their appearance is a most important item. In contrasting any shade of green against a warm colour, it should be remembered that the green containing most yellow must be opposed by a red having a blue or purple tone ; the true contrast of pure red being a decidedly blue hue of green.

The complementary colour of the bright green billiard-table-cloth is a rich purple-red, the two combined giving a very brilliant effect. Harmony of colour and brilliancy of contrast are not the principal objects in this instance ; the aim is rather to soften down the vivid green than to enhance its brightness, which would be done by any shade, however deep, of its complementary upon the walls. The best wall colour for the purpose will be a dull and soft-toned green, and by introducing the warm complementary colours into cornice and woodwork, pleasing and harmonious results will be obtained.

Notwithstanding the principles of colour-harmony are as definite as those which give us harmony of sound, a knowledge of the exact equivalents of a colour will not guarantee the successful colour-treatment of a room or building. Scientific equations should form the foundation of colour-studies ; but the amount of success obtained will depend upon adapting these definite laws to each particular circumstance and undertaking. In addition to the more obvious reasons that are mentioned, the climate and light, the position and interior lighting of the room, the scenery from the windows, are prominent factors in determining the strength and weakness of the contrasting tints which compose a harmonious colour scheme ; and it is under these conditions that mere scientific proportions fail the decorator, and he has to rely upon his own experience and faculty as a colourist.

CHAPTER II.
PIGMENTS.

IN the manufacture of pigments there are two actions, one chemical and the other mechanical; and there is a great difference between the two. In a chemical compound a substance is produced which differs from the several ingredients of which it is composed. A mechanical mixture, on the other hand, if put under a powerful microscope, reveals the fact that the atoms composing it are either unchanged or have altered merely in their shape, thus reflecting light in a different way.

The general qualities of good pigments are: beauty of colour, purity, brightness, and depth of colour, body, transparency, ease of manipulation, and durability. They should also keep their place, and dry or solidify well. Body in opaque pigments is the quality of colouring well; in transparent colours it means depth, richness of colour, or tinting power. Working well depends on either sufficient grinding, or fineness of texture, or the quality of the pigment. Keeping their place and drying well depend upon the liquid the colours are mixed with.

Sometimes there is a combined chemical and mechanical action in the production of a pigment. For instance, we may take the manufacture of vermilion—200 parts by weight of mercury, and 32 parts by weight of sulphur. When rubbed together in a mortar, the metallic lustre of the mercury and the yellow tone of the sulphur will disappear, and a grey powder (sulphide of mercury) will be the result. Now put this grey powder into a hard glass tube, closed at one end, then heat the closed end to a high temperature. The powder will be converted into a vapour, which will pass up and be deposited in the cooler part at the upper end of the tube. This operation is called sublimation. The sulphide of mercury thus treated is said to be sublimed. Let the tube be broken, and the deposit taken out and examined. It will then be found to be harder and blacker than the original grey sulphide. It also has a slight metallic lustre. Thus far it is chemical action; now comes the mechanical effect. When pounded in a mortar for some time, the pulverised substance becomes red. The more it is pounded the redder it becomes, because its particles are by this action more divided. Thus we find that two elements combined together become a greyish-black by chemical action; by altering its particles mechanically, it changes to a red.

Blue Black, as its name suggests, is a pigment of a blue hue of black. Its source is a charcoal obtained from the vine and other plants, cork-cuttings, and nut-shells, and its blue tone results from the thorough burning and levigation it goes through, as well as being due to the wood used in the first instance. It is very serviceable as a water-colour pigment, and is indispensable to distemper work generally, being used extensively as a graining colour. It produces soft grey shadows in some kinds of light woods; it also makes a fine neutral green with yellow, as its blue tone is useful for making low tones of green. It is very permanent, and acts best as a water-colour black. Although not much used as an oil stainer, it is, nevertheless, useful and reliable as such; its price is about 3d. per lb. retail, for the ordinary dry colour, up to 1s. 6d. for the finest qualities, in oil.

Ivory Black is at once the purest and blackest of all black pigments. Its name is derived from the supposition that it is—or was at one time—produced from burning ivory. The ordinary ivory black, however, is prepared by charring bones in closed vessels by a very strong heat. It is most often termed "drop black," and this by reason of its being usually sold in the form of drops, or knobs, when in its dry state. It is not very successful as a water-colour, but is a strong stainer in either oil or water. It is permanent in oil, and is most invaluable ground in turpentine for producing flat or dead black paint for various purposes, and mixes well with other pigments. Its price retail is from 8d. to 1s. per lb.

Lamp Black is, as its name implies, carbon given by the soot from resinous or oily flames, and is obtained for commercial purposes from factories where the preparation of turpentine and tar is carried on. It is a good black, but not so intense as "ivory," being more of the colour of Indian ink. It is very useful in either oil or water, and is quite permanent. It mixes well with most other pigments, but is spoilt if mixed with Prussian blue or Vandyke brown. It does not dry well.

Black Paint, as usually so termed, is a preparation of common blacks, but is ground in linseed oil to the form of a thick paste—very useful for common painting

Vegetable Black is an article similar to lamp black, and obtained by burning vegetable matter. It is wonderfully light, and therefore rather troublesome to mix and handle.

Besides these organic or burnt blacks, there are occasionally to be met with earth blacks, in the West of England and Wales, as well as black chalk, in their native condition. Generally speaking, they are not very pure in colour, nor do they exist in sufficient quantities to warrant considering them as ordinary black pigments.

Black Lead is a form of native pigment we all are familiar with, but, notwithstanding it possesses certain estimable qualities of permanence and purity, it is seldom looked upon as a painter's pigment.

Antwerp Blue is a preparation very similar both in source and qualities to Prussian blue; used as an oil glaze, it is somewhat brighter and greener, but it is neither so intense nor so permanent as the latter, either in oil or water.

Cobalt Blue is a pigment seldom used by house painters, owing to its costliness. It is second only to genuine ultramarine for beauty and purity of colour, and is much favoured for using as a sky blue, both in oil and water painting. It is not, however, nearly so strong a stainer as Prussian blue, but is thoroughly permanent and reliable in oil and water.

Indigo Blue is an ancient pigment of the nature of a dye, obtained from herbaceous plants which grow in India and other hot countries, and is usually sold dry in the form of little knobs. In its colour qualities and appearance it somewhat resembles Prussian blue, but is very inferior to that pigment for oil painting. It is for water-colour purposes that indigo is valuable. It is one of the most useful pigments for distemper tints that we have, and is just as permanent in water as it is unreliable in oil—that is, if good and pure indigo is used. The price, however, prevents its use to any great extent in house painting, being about four times as expensive as French ultramarine.

Indigo is also obtained by an electrolytic process, which gives it in the purest form obtainable. The dried plants are steeped in water, which becomes yellow in colour, and a current from copper electrodes is then made to pass through the liquid.

Prussian Blue is made from the action of prussiate of potash upon iron, the cyanide of the potash uniting with the iron producing the blue colour. If baked it becomes a brown; and when put upon a hot pan and roasted, if the hot pellets are then thrown into water and the colour is changed to a brown, this is through an alteration in the shape of its particles. It is a very interesting and curious thing that the colour of a substance can be thus changed by mechanical action.

It is a blue of much beauty and strength, not quite so pure as ultramarine, possessing a slight tinge of green, which, however, makes it none the less useful and beautiful for the painter's use. Some writers on the subject credit Prussian blue with the property of fluctuating—losing and gaining colour—according to the preponderance of oxygen in the air, although under all ordinary conditions it is quite reliable for oil painting. It gives very fine tints of blue in admixture with white lead; added to black in small quantities, it makes that neutral appear still more black and intense; whilst its brilliancy and transparency make it very useful for glazing over gold and silver leaf —a process so much used at the present time in decorating modern relief wall-hangings. Some notion of the strength of Prussian blue as a staining pigment may be gathered from the fact that ½ oz. ground in oil would stain 20 lbs. of white lead paint to a decided light blue. It is seldom used in water or distemper painting, as it does not show the same qualities of brilliancy and permanence as when used in oil. Its price is about that of good French ultramarine; it is always sold ground in oil or water, being too hard for the worker to grind or mix himself from its raw state.

Lime Blue, a cheap powder of somewhat similar colour to ultramarine, comes next in order of usefulness, but far less pure and strong as a stainer. As its name implies, it is useful only for mixing with water preparations of chalk-lime or whiting (carbonate of lime), and is much used by the paper-stainer for cheap goods. It is practically useless for oil paint. A fair quality should be retailed at 6d. per lb.

Royal Blue is a finely-ground cobalt: that is to say, it is ground in a glass tinted with cobalt, which is disintegrated by plunging it whilst hot into cold water.

Ultramarine Blue is by far the most pure and costly of all pigments in our use and knowledge, and has been known and used from the time of the first Pharaohs. Its name is derived from the Latin *ultra*, beyond, and *mare*, the sea; and by the ancient Greeks it was known as Armenian blue. The real colour is made from a precious stone, which is, however, destroyed in the process. This stone, called lapis-lazuli, is of a beautiful azure colour, marked with fine golden veins, and is principally obtained from Persia and Siberia. Four qualities of genuine ultramarine blue are quoted in colourmen's catalogues, the prices ranging from £3 3s. to £7 17s. 6d. *per ounce*. But we can get ultramarine at all manner of prices. We can get manufactured ultramarine at 5d. per lb.; lime blue is the cheapest form. These commercial substitutes for real ultramarine are more suitable for water colour than oil, as they rapidly absorb water: if used with oil, they should be well dried before mixing.

Factitious *Ultramarine* is, however, a commodity that most painters are familiar with. It is prepared artificially in a great number of qualities, and retailed, consequently, at an equal variety of prices. It is always sold in the form of a fine powder, at prices ranging from 1s. 6d. to 3s. 6d. per lb. for house-painters' use. It is a most useful pigment, possessing much purity and brilliancy, is permanent, and can be mixed with either oil or distemper paints.

Blue Verditer, a preparation of copper, is a very pure and pretty light blue. As it is serviceable only in water, and is not thoroughly permanent, its use is chiefly confined to the paper-stainers.

Vandyke Brown is an earth, consisting of iron and bituminous coal. It is a deep rich brown, useful to a degree in pictures or in graining; with oil it is a bad drier. It is not a very permanent colour, and is rather mischievous to the other colours.

Chrome Yellow is made by mixing bichromate of potash with acetate of lead, or, as it is commercially called, sugar-of-lead. It is also made commercially by staining whiting with the bichromate. This is done to give it a body; the lead is boiled in bichromate of potash. On the duration of time of the boiling depends whether it is lemon, deep, or middle chrome. Soda is also used in the above process to produce red chrome. It is easy to see that this colour should not be used with zinc-white. Chrome tints look very rich with browns or purples, but chrome colours are fugitive.

Yellow and Orange Chromes are very often adulterated. In the pure state they consist of chromate of lead or of chromate and sulphate of lead.

Pale Chromes.—The great desideratum is to obtain a pale shade with the least quantity of sulphuric acid, or what amounts to the same thing, the minimum of paleness with the maximum of staining power. As the shade deepens the strength lessens; the orange chromes often contain orange lead, which is very objectionable.

Medium Chromes should give a clear golden tone with white lead, and not a buff. A fourth or third of zinc white mixed with the white lead holds the colour better. The pale shades ought not to approach green; the grinding should be very fine, without any trace of grit.

Gamboge is a transparent colour, only useful for glazing, lacquers, or for transparency painting, or for water-colours.

Green pigments, chiefly derived from the mineral sources of copper, are very plentiful and reasonable in price. Brunswick greens, quaker greens, chrome greens, etc., are all useful pigments, owing their colour to their preparation from the same mineral sources as Prussian blue and chromes. Generally, it may be granted that they are reliable and fairly permanent for their cost— about 3d. to 6d. per lb. retail; but the painter will do well to avoid their use for tints with white lead in good and permanent interior work.

Bronze, olive, and invisible greens are, as their names imply, deep but richly-toned pigments, very useful for external painting and very reasonable in price. They can be almost as easily mixed by compounding black and yellow pigments, or black, blue, and green, according to the particular hue or cast that may be desired.

Emerald Green is made from arsenic. In oil it is permanent; when dry, it is so dusty and poisonous that there is danger in mixing it with water. It is a very assertive colour, unharmonious and harsh. It is best to make up green with yellow and blue rather than use emerald green decoratively. A beautiful neutral green can be made by mixing yellow and black.

Paris green is a crystalline colour, and its richness of tint depends upon this. In grinding, a colour of very fine crystal must be selected. To test this colour for purity, dissolve out the oil by means of benzine, and dry

c

the residue, then treat it with strong ammonia ; if pure, it will entirely dissolve.

Verdigris is a transparent green, and, like the last colour, is a copper compound entirely soluble in ammonia.

Madder Lake from the plant is the most permanent of the lake colours. That made from the cochineal insects with salts of tin is not so permanent. The Venetians used to lay on their lakes without admixture over the plaster of Paris ground spoken of on p. 40, and even then locked in the colour by a rim of varnish, to protect it from the contamination of any other colour. The old Persians would take a rug, dip it in a preparation of madder and milk, and then lay it in the hot sunshine, thus fixing it, and giving it a beautiful colour. It is the modern dyer who takes the insect cochineal, and reducing tin with an acid produces a red exceedingly brilliant, but not so beautiful as the old Persian red. Madder lake is more permanent. This cochineal colour does not harmonise so readily with other colours, and is not so lasting as madder.

Ochres.—For all purposes of house painting, the yellow ochres are the most useful. They are an earth, and owe their colour to hydrated oxide of iron, and vary in tint according to the amount of the latter present; they are, in fact, clays coloured by hydrated oxide of iron, and therefore contain silicate of alumina and silica. Ochres are found in a native state in most countries, and plentifully in our own, the best coming from Oxfordshire and Derbyshire.

The tone of ochre ranges from pale yellow to brown, and there are several shades of red, as well as some other tones, produced by burning.

From the earliest days of history, ochres have been known and used, being of good body, and very reliable, if suitably prepared, for both oil and water painting. The variety of tone and shade in which they are to be found is endless, and to the action of iron is due the colour of them all. As all varieties of ochre can be produced artificially and cheaply from iron, and since all native pigments require grinding and washing before being fit for painting, it need scarcely be added that the bulk of such yellow pigments used are of the manufactured kind. For making with white the very serviceable straw, stone, and buff tints for large plain surfaces, and the grounds for graining the ochres are quite indispensable. Ochre is too cheap for adulteration, but it varies in staining power and in its tone. It is sometimes mixed with bad oil, and in other cases is not sufficiently washed. It is a permanent colour, and harmless to the other colours. In oil it requires driers.

The value of an ochre does not depend upon the amount of oxide of iron present, but upon the purity of the tint. Good ochre is invariably a mixture of ochre and chrome yellow.

The French ochres, which are the finest, are regarded as standards of quality.

Purple-Brown, is itself an oxide of iron. Iron is treated with lime and acid to produce it. It is very permanent in itself, but weakens tints with which it is mixed, not because it chemically destroys the other colours, but because it retains its own strength, whilst the others fade. As its name implies, it is the lowest in the scale of brightness, being, in fact, a dense brown. It is most in demand for external painting, when it forms the basis of most so-called chocolate hues. Although not being useful for admixture with white—muddiness resulting—it presents in mass a comfortable-looking appearance, used alone, in oil or water processes.

Red Lead is a preparation of burnt massicol (an oxide of lead), of a bright scarlet colour. Although, if used by itself in oil or varnish, it will retain its brightness for some time, it is useless for mixing tints, and is destructive to other colours when mixed with them. It is altogether useless, too, with water, which turns it black. It is, however, well adapted for priming, or first coat, either alone or mixed with white lead, and is a great preservative to wood and iron. Being a good drier it is used for hardening white lead, when mixed as a putty or as paint for preservative purposes. Red lead is an important pigment, and as a paint is the best preservative that can be used. It should never be mixed with whiting or similar bodies, but oxide of iron may be used in conjunction with it to advantage.

Red Ochres comprise the most valuable, and also the cheapest, red pigments in general use ; the best of these, for house-painting purposes, being Venetian and Indian reds and purple-brown.

All these reds having, if properly mixed and used, sufficient covering power to hide, in one coat, almost any other coloured surface, they are, therefore, very useful and economical for preservative and plain painting in such a climate as our own. Although existing in a native condition, these commercial reds are usually manufactured pigments—viz., burnt ochres. They are sold in powder form, but Venetian red and purple-brown are generally to be had ready ground in linseed oil. Vermilion and Indian red, from the reason of their more heavy nature, would soon become solidly caked, and, therefore, are only ground in oil or turpentine when so ordered. Of course, this does not apply to colours in collapsible tubes. Venetian red, Indian red, Turkey red, rose-pink, and red oxide owe their colour almost entirely to oxide of iron.

Indian Red, originally coming from Bengal, is a rich deep red, of slightly purple tone, with all the good qualities of body and permanence of its preceding pigment. Of late years, the supply of that brilliant and rosy-toned pigment which we originally knew as Indian red appears to have been exhausted, its place now being taken—or, rather, its name usurped—by the comparatively dull and muddy reds of artificial source. There is, however, a good variety obtained from the Forest of Dean ; it is a beautiful colour in itself, and is a splendid stainer. It has a purple hue, and is very permanent and satisfactory.

Indian reds cannot be classed as pure if they contain less than 95 per cent. of oxide ; the paler the colour, the greater is its tinting strength, and rosier the tint; the deep-coloured give purplish tints.

Turkey red is essentially a mixture of Indian red with a lake colour or with rose-pink. The object to be sought for in Turkey red is its brilliancy, and next its opacity, or body. It should also be very finely ground.

Venetian Red is a natural red ochre, with more iron in it than the other ochres; it consists usually of oxide of iron and sulphate of lime. Its comparative brightness must be examined, and also fineness of grinding. It is of good body, makes clean tints with white in both oil and water, and is sufficiently cheap for any purpose. It is permanent; but there is an imitation, made from vitriol, which is not so permanent, and is altogether unsatisfactory.

Vermilion is a mineral sulphide of mercury, pre-eminent for its brilliancy and purity of red, and is one of the pigments known and used by the ancients. Although it may be found in a native state, principally in China and California (requiring grinding, however, before being fit for use), the vermilion of commerce is principally an article manufactured from mercury. It is a crystalline pigment. The larger the crystal, the deeper the tint, therefore the paler shades have most body. Sulphide of mercury is found in the earth. It formerly came from China; and Chinese vermilion has the reputation of being the best, although the English manufactured article nearly, but not quite, reaches it. The natural sulphide is called, commercially, cinnabar.

The quality of it varies very much. It presents a splendid field for the enterprising adulterator. To find out if it is pure, put a portion on a hot metal plate, and hold it over a flame. If genuine, it will practically disappear when sufficiently heated; the extent of the adulteration will be apparent by the amount which remains. It is seldom in much request for house painting in its full strength, being too vivid for the light, climate, and social sentiments of this country; and being also very heavy, and ranging from 3s. 6d. to

5s. 6d. per lb. retail, it is too costly for large surfaces. Vermilion is, however, very useful for obtaining, with white, pure and clean pink, and similar delicate tints, which are permanent; if required in its full brilliancy, vermilion stands best with, and applied in, good oil varnish alone. Imitation vermilions are made from orange lead coloured with eosin. Crimson tones are obtained by admixture with white lead, zinc-white, sulphate of lead, etc. Cheap colours are made from red lead and barytes.

Siennas are in their nature much the same as ochres, but contain more iron in their composition. They possess in a high degree the nature of getting brighter and yellower by age and exposure. They have a greater staining power than ochre, and are slow in drying.

Burnt Sienna. Although coming more under the heading of red pigments, by reason of its bright, if impure, orange-red, this is, as its name implies, a burnt preparation of the mother pigment. By the latter process it gains also in transparency and staining power, and it is really indispensable when graining some kinds of wood. It is obtained by baking the raw sienna till it becomes a rich orange-brown, with great transparency and depth of colour. It has all the excellent qualities of ochre and raw sienna, with this addition: that it dries a little quicker.

Terra di Sienna, or Raw Sienna, is a very useful pigment. Although not so clean and bright in yellow as good ochre, it has more staining power when used with white, with which it forms very soft and agreeable cream tints and the so-called "ivory whites," so much in demand of late years. It is obtainable ready ground both in oil or in water, is equally serviceable in either case, and is reasonable in price. For the imitation of maple, satinwood, pitch pine, etc., it is very popular and useful, prepared in water, whilst its semi-transparent nature renders it valuable where transparent effects are desired in oil painting processes.

Terra Vert is a silicate earth, permanent and slightly

transparent either in oil or water. It is used extensively for the peculiar tone of flesh needed in painting figures, because of its neutral tone.

The *Umbers* contain iron and manganese; they are useful colours, containing all the virtues and all the usefulness possible. The most common is usually termed raw umber—a natural ochre, found almost all over the world. The best is Turkey umber, and this, after burning, which makes it richer and warmer—when it is known as burnt umber—is one of the most useful pigments. For graining it is almost indispensable, and for all general purposes of painters' and paper-stainers' work it is one of the most valuable aids to soft and modest colouring, both in oil and water processes, we possess. Its price varies, according to quality and preparation, from $\frac{1}{2}$d. to 1s. per pound.

Whiting is carbonate of lime; it should be used only with the earth pigments, as it has a tendency to destroy vegetable colours. Prussian blue, Brunswick and the cochineal lakes, and most of the yellows are of little use when mixed with whiting. Ochres, umbers, siennas, blue-black, Venetian and Indian red, vermilion, madder, and most of the blues, are useful with whiting. It is the pigment which is used for wall papers, so that there should not be any difficulty in getting an extensive range of colours to go with it, as we know the number of tones used in wall papers is unlimited.

White lead—white oxide of lead—is mixed with almost all other colours, sometimes to their detriment. It is very durable, and is, in consequence, a good preservative; it is the strongest of all whites in opacity or covering power. When genuine, and properly prepared for use, it is a very reliable agent in obtaining a successfully painted surface—viz., a compact and pleasing incrustation — which, under fair conditions, maintains its colour and is impervious to water for a great number of years. Now for its disadvantages. It is highly poisonous, but the poison is very eccentric in its effect. The health of some people is not at all injured by its use, whilst that of others is affected by the slightest contact with it. Food should not be eaten in the presence of lead, especially when it is in the process of evaporation. An instance has occurred where a whole family have been poisoned by drinking water drawn from a tank that had received several coats of white lead paint. Acid drinks and milk are good antidotes. When using lead, painters should take as much oil before going to bed at night as they can digest—a teaspoonful or less. Of course, the utmost cleanliness is very necessary. The acid of fruit helps to check the deleterious action of lead. An acid drink is an excellent antidote. Citric acid or acetic acid in water, or drink made from lemons, are very good. It is the acid principle rather than the particular acid.

Then as to its effect on colour: it is so deleterious that for grounds the great Venetian painters never used it. The Venetian painters prepared a ground of plaster of Paris. We may be certain that if we start with white lead—a mineral—and put any vegetable colour with it, we shall find the mineral kill the vegetable. The safest way to use colours so that they are not destroyed is to use only mineral with mineral colours, and only vegetable with vegetable colours. White lead is not suitable for water colour, as it goes black when used without oil. Age gives white lead a yellow tinge, and damp will turn it black. If coated over dark colours, it will sink into them, and the darker colour will show through. There are instances of this in old pictures. Raphael, after painting a red cap on a figure in one of his pictures, desired to do without the cap, and so painted it out with a colour whose principal part consisted of lead. After a time the cap came through, and now shows; of course, not so bright as it originally was, but like the ghost of the cap.

The ordinary process of obtaining white lead is by the slow corrosion of small castings of metallic lead, caused by its exposure over acid in small earthenware vessels.

This is known as the Dutch method, and it requires at least ninety days for the corrosion, which, of course, adds to the price to no small extent, especially as considerable time is required, in addition, for the lead to mature. During the past few years, however, there have been patented from time to time a number of new processes, most of them having for their immediate object the saving of time in manufacture. A successful American invention has been introduced into this country, by the processes of which the dressed ore is volatilised by heat, the resulting fumes are carried forward by air currents, and ultimately solidified, instead of escaping into the atmosphere; the end of which is that, after necessary refining purposes are completed, there remains a fine, sublimated white lead, which has been obtained without the escape of any poisonous fumes, and presented fit for practical use without any particular danger to the health of those engaged in its manufacture. One of the results of using white lead that is too fresh is "chalking"—*i.e.*, powdering of the lead under the action of atmosphere. Of the new processes of corrosion that have been successful, the most interesting is probably that in which the metallic lead is reduced to particles as fine as powder, and then subjected to the action of acid, which reduces it in a short time to hydro-carbonate of lead.

The manufacture is, of course, attended with considerable danger to the operatives, the degree of which certainly depends somewhat upon workshop sanitation, medical precautions, and on individual constitutions, but which, in any case, is sufficiently serious to render it most urgent that a substitute be found. There are authenticated instances of reckless employés reaching an average old age, whilst more careful livers suffer in all stages—from ordinary sickness and debility up to partial paralysis or the torture of death by gradual yet virulent poisoning.

The baneful results of lead poisoning are not peculiar to the people actually employed in white lead factories, but will be found also to a very large extent among paint-grinders and painters generally. Men have become confirmed invalids and cripples through the effects of lead in their systems ; strong, healthy young men have been attacked, and incapacitated from work for as long as fourteen and fifteen weeks at a time, through the effects of what is known in the trade as lead colic.

The question of an efficient substitute for white lead is, therefore, one of literally vital importance. It has been frequently asserted that there is no substitute for it ; that a pigment cannot be made that will answer the purpose, having all the advantages claimed for the carbonate of lead. Certainly, sulphate of lead has not the body or covering properties that carbonate of lead has ; but there are other white pigments. For instance, oxide of zinc can claim to be one of the best white paints in the market, and it has certainly a decided advantage over white lead, inasmuch as it is not the least injurious to health, and retains its colour under all atmospheric conditions. But there, again, body is wanting. But it would be far preferable to use an article that we know has no pernicious effects than one we know is most deadly. There is also another pigment—sulphide of zinc—which has a greater advantage still ; while being cheaper than oxide of zinc, it has a much better body and as great a covering power as carbonate of lead. It was first introduced by the Silicate Paint Company, of Charlton, in Kent, some fourteen or fifteen years ago, and their sales are said to have steadily increased, until they now reach several thousand tons annually, notwithstanding that there are other firms manufacturing a somewhat similar article.

Mr. Laurie's paper on White Lead Substitutes, read before the Society of Arts in January, 1894, states that, so far as the author knows, sulphate of lead and oxide of lead are the only efficient substitutes available. Zinc oxide is in very general use in Japan and in France. Its merit is greatest in point of long-retained whiteness, and its defect in covering power. Zinc oxide is known commercially as "zinc white," lead sulphate as "Glasgow sulphate" and "Freeman's white." When zinc oxide is ground up with lead sulphate under heavy edge runners, the covering power of the compound is considerably greater than that of either component if applied separately. Laboratory experiments made by Mr. Laurie show that the quantity wanted for three successive coats is about equal when either the mixture named, or Freeman's white, or white lead is used: sublimed oxide of zinc requires rather more. The relative quantities of oil required are about the same. The colour value is distinctly greater in the case of the substitutes; whilst there can be only one opinion respecting the value of this freedom from the dangers peculiar to white lead: it is open to question whether this is an altogether desirable quality. Probably few persons outside the trade are aware that by use of white lead paint they have in their houses a sensitive detector of poisonous sewer gas—a sanitary quality of which most of the "sanitary enamels" that are now the rage are, by reason of the entire absence of lead in their composition, almost or entirely destitute. In practical house painting, zinc-white is often used in obtaining the finest white surfaces for enamelling and hand polishing of wood-work. Since this class of work is of a very laborious and expensive nature, it naturally follows that a pigment should be used which maintains its colour for a great number of years.

In *Charlton White* we possess a *zinc white* which has the body of white lead without its drawbacks. It has also its covering power. Although it works a little drier than does white lead, yet it makes purer decorative tints, and is not discoloured by suphuretted hydrogen present in foul air. It is a fine colour for inside work, and is not poisonous. Although this article is scarcely likely to supersede white lead for general purposes, it is rapidly getting a wider reputation. Its elementary sources are said to be barytes, strontium, and zinc; its market value is about the same as the best white lead. Till a method was found out to give a body to zinc white during the process of manufacture, it was only used to finish work with, as it was formerly so transparent in its nature, though always a better white than white lead. Zinc white and white lead paints mixed together will not agree, but will destroy any painting. Work is sometimes got up in white lead and finished with zinc white, and they will work well this way; but the two are never mixed in one coat of colour.

Flake White, Nottingham White, Silver White, etc., are all preparations of metallic lead, differing in process of manufacture and minor resultant qualities, but are not necessary here to be further considered.

The ordinary white lead for painting is obtained, ground to the form of a thick paste, in linseed oil, the heaviest and whitest being the best. It is, as a commercial article, extensively adulterated with sulphate of baryta, whiting, etc.; and it follows, therefore, that the surest way of obtaining it genuine is by purchase from a vendor or firm of reliable reputation, and to be willing to pay a fair price, according to the fluctuations of the market.

Zinc White.—Oxide of zinc is a very useful pigment, being permanent in both oil and water. To no extent, however, does it rival, for general use, the oxides of lead, since it is vastly inferior in body—covering power—to genuine white lead. Its principal merit is found in the fact of its being entirely free from the dangerous attributes, both during preparation and use, which attend the handling of white lead.

The subject of colour testing is one that might profitably be studied by all painters, paint-makers, and merchants.

The following scheme is one given by A. Wilson in a paper read before the Association of Master Painters and Decorators:—

Colours are examined for (1) purity of material; (2) purity of tone, brilliancy, or richness; (3) fineness of grinding; (4) spreading capacity or covering power; (5) body, or power to conceal the substance which it coats; (6) staining power, or tinting strength, when mixed with white or other colours; (7) quality or purity of tint with white; (8) if a paste colour, the consistency of the paste; (9) transparency of transparent colours.

Pigments are very frequently adulterated, calcium sulphate or gypsum and silica being often used; for instance, gypsum in Venetian red and silica in ochre. White clay, or kaolin, is also very frequently used, but clay occurs naturally in such pigments as ochre, sienna, amber, Vandyke brown, and earths generally. Carbonate of lime or chalk is also used as an adulterant. It occurs naturally in some pigments, but only in very small quantities. It is often mixed with white lead. In some colours, such as rose-pink, chalk is used as a vehicle for carrying the colour, and its use in these is therefore admissible. Barytes, when mixed with oil, is devoid of opacity and covering power; when mixed with pigments that are specifically lighter, it will separate after painting into two layers, the barytes being in the lower. Whiting and gypsum are better oil absorbents than barytes. Oxide of zinc, owing to its certainty to chip off, will never replace white lead, but it may be used as a finishing coat to the latter.

Green Pigments.—The green most used is that known as chrome green. It consists of a mixture of Prussian blue and chrome yellow, and is often prepared by precipitation of the two substances simultaneously from solution. The commercial chrome greens consist usually of about one part colour and three parts mineral white (generally barytes). They may conveniently be divided into two classes—those inclining to yellow and those inclining to blue in tint.

For testing these pigments, three standards, in three different shades of perfectly pure greens, are used. By mixing two of these standard greens, any desired tint may be obtained.

If it were desired to test an oxide paint, the most practical way would be an examination as to colour and degree of fineness in grinding. This refers to the oxide in paste form, and not diluted with oils for use, as in the latter case the oil would be a factor of importance, whether good "honest linseed" or "fishy" oil, in the twofold sense. Oxide paint is so cheap, there is no need to adulterate it, although there are several qualities of colour (brightness) and fineness. In actual use the oil is more the preservative than the oxide, which is rather a *cheap* body pigment with affinity for iron-work.

To tell whether any sample of paint is lead or zinc, put it into the flame of a gas-burner. If it is lead, it will turn brown by the action of the sulphuretted hydrogen of the gas; if it is zinc, it will keep white, and be unaffected.

Barytes, chalk, china, clay, and gypsum are the substances used to adulterate white lead. There are also samples of lead which are imperfectly made, and either badly washed or not ground sufficiently to be perfect.

To find out what substance any sample of lead is adulterated with would necessitate the use of a chemical laboratory, but a few simple tests may be of use to enable anyone to tell pure white lead.

White lead should not incline to pink or grey, nor be gritty. These are evidences of faults in the manufacture. There are some people who hold that barytes improves lead; but it is a question whether it is so or no. A good way to test as to adulteration is to rub a portion of lead in a little sulphuric acid on a piece of glass with a bone palette-knife; if it is free from adulteration, and a good lead, it will mix to a smooth paste. For a very strong and absolute test, take a piece of white lead, mix it up to the consistency of flatting with turps, let it stand till the lead settles, then pour off the turps, and add some benzine to it; then stir it well and shake it up, and let it settle again till next day. Then pour off the benzine, and place the white lead upon a piece of blotting-paper; you will then have your sample in a state of dry white lead. Dissolve this in a little dilute nitric acid. If any sediment at all remains then, this will be the substance used for adulteration.

CHAPTER III.

OILS, DRIERS, VARNISHES, ETC.

WE will now briefly occupy ourselves with those fluids which are indispensable to the worker for compounding with pigments mixed in paint.

Oils are usually divided into two classes, and are termed fixed oils and volatile oils. Fixed oils are further distinguished, by their nature and source, into fat oils and drying oils. Fat oils are those which contain an excess of oleic acid, or stearine, as the animal and fish oils, and these are consequently non-drying oils. Drying oils are those which harden into a solid form : as, for instance, linseed, poppy, and nut oils.

Good and reliable fluids are as necessary in the mixing of paint as are good pigments. Linseed oil occupies a position amongst oils similar to that taken by genuine white lead amongst the solids; and just as white lead forms the basis in nearly all light colour paints, so linseed is the principal solvent in the preparation of varnishes and other vehicles.

The source and appearance of linseed oil are familiar to most people; but its qualities and properties, from a painter's point of view, are matters it is necessary to consider here. Drying oils, and linseed oil particularly, amongst that class, owe the characteristic of drying to their excess of resinous properties, and therefore, when used under the influence of oxygen, they dry or harden into a film of horny substance.

Linseed oil, then, is the most useful of all oils for the painter, but it turns to a yellow-brown colour rapidly, and darkens by age. To help to prevent this, turpentine is mixed with the colour, and it is best to use the oil sparingly when mixing paint, for the reason that in drying it darkens the lead. Colour and smell are the tests for good oil (some painters even taste it). A good way is to compare the odour with that of crushed linseed meal. By mentioning that animal oils are turned brown by chlorine and that vegetable oils remain colourless, a test is revealed for any oils whose nature is unascertained.

The few of the imperfections common to good linseed oil do not materially affect the work of the house-painter. But it should be of good quality. It should always be transparent, free from any rancid smell or taste, and of a light yellow or amber colour. A well-stocked market of linseed supplies our wants at a very reasonable price, and there is little occasion for using any of the other expressed oils.

Boiled Oil—that is, boiled linseed oil—is a very serviceable preparation which must be noticed. Boiled oil is the ultimate product of the raw linseed oil boiled with *litharge*, or some similar matter. By this process the oxidising or drying qualities of the litharge are communicated to the oil, which furthermore gains body and brilliancy. The boiling of linseed oil causes it to become much darker, and hence it is seldom used for light colours, and but rarely for interior painting. For preservative work, boiled oil is almost indispensable, and especially with dark pigments; its colour is then no disadvantage, whilst its extra body and hardening qualities are a decided gain. In the process of manufacturing boiled oil, raw linseed oil is brought up to the boiling point, a little manganese being steeped in it during the boiling; it thus becomes the boiled oil of commerce. Badly-boiled oil has the fault of ropiness. It should be nearly as limpid as raw oil, and should, if spread on a piece of glass, either dry or rapidly have a skin over it.

Gilders' Fat Oil is linseed oil in another condition, and is the chief factor used in making gilders' and decorators' *oil gold size*. It may be prepared by keeping raw oil in a closed vessel for a considerable length of time, by which it acquires a special brilliancy and drying quality; then it is prepared as oil gold size with certain pigments. Good fat oil for gilding has been made by keeping the accumulated skins and scrapings of gold size in a clay jar, and then adding sufficient best raw oil to cover them. Being exposed to the atmosphere, but protected from rain, etc., for about a year, with occasional stirring, the oil, by the oxidising action of the old size-skins and the exposure to air, has been converted into good fat oil. Doubtless, there are more expeditious ways of artificially preparing it, but the above gives a fairly quick and reliable result.

Like linseed oil, turpentine is largely used in the manufacture of varnishes and other painters' vehicles.

Oil of Turpentine, commonly called *turps* and sometimes, but incorrectly, termed *spirit* of turpentine, has a colourless appearance and strong pungent odour, as well as an inflammable nature, doubtless familiar to most readers. Turpentine contains a slight proportion of resin and other matter which will not evaporate by exposure or heat: which fact demonstrates the fallacy of calling it a spirit; but its volatile nature makes it invaluable to the painter for thinning the drying oils and for making "flatting" paint. Since oil of turpentine contains but a small proportion of the resinous properties common to the expressed oils, it follows that its binding quality is very poor; and paint compounded with turps alone can be rubbed away by friction.

There are several methods of testing turpentine, and the points upon which it is possible to tell its purity are:—(1) The specific gravity; (2) the boiling-point; (3) the action upon polarised light; (4) the absence of fluorescence; (5) the residue on evaporation. Turpentine is sometimes adulterated by the addition of paraffin oil.

Varnishing is the last process of house-painting, and consists in covering the pigments with a film of a transparent resinous nature, which not only preserves the paint from the ill effects of the atmosphere and handling, but brings out the colour of the pigment to its fullest extent. Where paint is prepared with an excess of raw linseed or boiled oil, varnishing is not necessary, since the oil itself encases and protects the particles of the pigment or solid used, and by its smoothness and body maintains a good gloss. With better-class work, and graining and marbling, a protective body of oil varnish is desirable, but experience and knowledge are necessary to discriminate between the varied kinds that are made.

As varnishes come to the painter, it is quite impossible that he should know the composition of the material he is using; only the reputation of the maker can be his guide, as the varnishes that are made owe their excellence to the exactness and perfection of their manufacture.

The skill needed in their manufacture is often acquired by a generation of careful experiment and practice. Although the best of varnishes are made from gums, yet the excellence of the varnish is a great deal due to the process of manufacture; and although varnish is made by melting the gum in raw linseed oil, yet to put oil to varnish once made would destroy its drying power. In a case where a painter put oil into the varnish for a dado of many yards' extent to make his work less hard, the result was that nothing would make it dry; it had to be washed off.

Varnishes may be considered in three classes: as expressed oil varnishes, volatile oil varnishes, and spirit varnishes; and from these terms some notion of the solvents or liquids they are compounded from is gathered. It is customary to further distinguish them by the substance or resin they contain, such as copal varnish and mastic varnish, and again by their probable use, as oak varnish and maple varnish.

For whatever purpose varnish is required, it is most unwise for a novice to attempt to prepare it himself. When a painter's apprentice was necessarily initiated into the making of boiled oil, japanners' gold size, etc., the price of varnish was high and excused the experiment; but nowadays the attempt can only be considered, under ordinary circumstances, as a *dangerous* waste of time and material. Keen competition has reduced varnish making to a matter of fair profits, and briefly considering here the substances from which they are compounded will tend to the better and more intelligent use of the varnishes.

The most serviceable varnishes for use in connection with painting belong to *oil varnishes*, and these are usually *copal*—the name given to the gum principally used in their manufacture. Copal gum in appearance somewhat resembles amber, and it is imported from the tropics. When varnish makers purchase a parcel of gums, the pieces are very carefully assorted into various degrees of lightness and transparency. The whitest variety of the gum is usually the scarcest; and as it follows that the colour of the copal must exercise a considerable influence over that of the ultimate product, white copal varnish is consequently found a most expensive preparation.

Generally, in the manufacture of copal varnishes, the gum is first dissolved by heat and then converted by turpentine into the liquid form, with the addition of linseed oil, to give the copal elasticity. The colour of the oil used is, therefore, a further important factor. Colourless varnish, such as that known as *mastic*, can be made by simply dissolving picked gum mastic in oil of turpentine; but since the absence of linseed oil causes the liquid to set and harden very rapidly, such a preparation would be practically useless for the house-painter, besides lacking in that elasticity and body which it is the special property of linseed oil to contribute.

For the house-painter's finest interior work, white oil varnish—that is, a liquid which can be spread and worked upon broad surfaces, and such as will dry in about eight hours—is very requisite. Various eminent firms make such a varnish for decorators and painters, and sell it under fanciful names. The chief attributes aimed at are freedom from yellowness and the possession of good "hand-polishing" qualities. The price of such a white interior varnish would be from 20s. to 30s. per gallon to the trade.

In addition to this polishing varnish, a maker's list usually contains one or two varieties of what are termed *superfine copal* varnishes. These range in price from 16s. to 20s. per gallon, possessing different names and features, such as "polishing" and "extra hard-drying."

Lower down in the scale of costliness will be found the best kinds of ordinary *copal varnish*. Many varieties are made of this quality, and for such purposes as the names *inside copal* and *outside copal* suggest to the purchasers. The prices of these range from 12s. to 16s. per gallon.

The varnishes usually termed *cheap oaks* in the trade are generally of a most serviceable class, and can be purchased, suitable for all kinds of interior and external surfaces, at from 8s. to 12s. per gallon.

Quality is *the* essential consideration in a varnish. The prices given above are more for relative comparison than as any guide to purchasers: but they are well representative of the best makers' current prices.

Preparations of coarse oil and common resins are placed upon the market at much lower prices; but the inexperienced especially should always purchase an established maker's goods through a reliable retailer.

There are yet a few other varieties to mention; and of these, a good friend is *hard drying* or *church oak* varnish, although in copal oak varnish quickness of hardening must generally be accompanied by a tendency to lose gloss and to crack, from excess of resin. A preparation known under the above names is always to be had for seats of public buildings, stained floors, and common furniture, for which it is most valuable. This make of varnish, retailed at about 16s. per gallon, is also used for kitchen furniture; since, unlike many and even expensive painters' varnishes, it does not get soft and sticky by the warmth of the body, whilst its oily nature makes it very durable. The litharge or similar substance with which it is prepared, however, considerably darkens the oil, so that this would not do for light-coloured paint.

Maple Varnish is but another name for a good quality of interior copal varnish, made from the palest gums and refined oil, so that when coated over such delicate figure as the imitation of maple and satin-wood, it shall not disadvantageously affect the colour of the grainer's work beneath.

The varnishing of *wall papers* is an important item of painters' work, and covering the walls of middle-class houses with pattern papers suitable for varnishing on staircase, bath-room, and kitchen walls especially, is a commendable and growing practice, consistent alike with sanitation, durability, and decorative effect. For use on all paper hangings on which the yellowness of copal varnish would not be detrimental to the colour of the design, a good quality of this variety is far preferable to the paper varnishes sold by the manufacturing houses. Whether used upon walls or wood-work, the colour of copal oak varnish would spoil such tints as French or green-greys, delicate pinks or white; but for "terra-cotta" shades, buffs, leather, or cinnamon colours, the yellowness would be no disadvantage.

Where white paper varnish is necessary, that which is termed crystal paper or fine pale paper varnish is used. The first is the whitest; and as it can contain but little linseed oil, it requires very expeditious and experienced working when used over large surfaces. Crystal paper, copal cabinet, and quick furniture varnishes come under the heading of volatile oil varnishes; so does mastic varnish, used for varnishing papers, maps, etc. Genuine mastic varnish costs about 50s. per gallon, but the cheap substitutes given above range from 14s. to 20s., trade price.

White hard and *brown hard spirit varnish* are the two most useful amongst the purely *spirit varnishes*. They are similar in nature to French polish, all being prepared from various kinds of *lac*—shel-lac, etc.—and spirits of wine, or methylated spirit. The lustre they give is nearer to that of French polish, and "softer" than that given by a copal oil: hence white hard and brown hard are much used for furniture as a substitute for the more tedious process of French polishing, and also upon those portions where the polisher's rubber could not be used; they cost about 8s. per gallon.

Bath Varnish is a very hard-drying white liquid, similar in nature to the "enamels" now on the market, but is a more durable article, and resists the action of hot water to a greater extent than the other preparations. Its price is about 20s. per gallon.

There are a few *vehicles* and liquids used by painters which scarcely come under the heading of oils and varnishes. The word varnish is so associated with a glossy surface, that the name flatting or lustreless varnish, given to a preparation of oil of turpentine, copal, and wax, is somewhat a misnomer. This is not often called for, since it possesses very little body; but upon timbered and ornamental wooden ceilings it can be used with decided advantage over ordinary copal, the small amount of wax gloss it gives out being far more restful and natural for such positions than a bright hard glitter.

Black Japan is a species of black copal varnish, made in various qualities, and the best being that for carriage painting. House-painters seldom use it for other than blacking grates or iron-work, although there are many other purposes for which it can be used. Thinned down with turps, it makes a capital stain of a rich brown colour for wood.

Berlin Black is another preparation useful for various purposes, as it is a dense black, drying with only an egg-shell gloss; like Brunswick black, it is prepared chiefly for iron-work. Cheaper black varnishes, similar in nature to Brunswick, are also to be purchased at 4s. per gallon.

Varnish Stains are liquids of similar nature and preparation to brown hard spirit varnish, but are coloured with permanent vegetable dyes, to represent, when spread on clean white wood, the various colours of oak, walnut, mahogany, etc. When applied without any previous preparation, two coats are necessary to get a glossy effect upon new wood. As a varnish and stain combined, they are most useful and convenient for picture-frames, fretwork, and other little matters.

Patent Knotting, or *Knotting Composition*, is a brown spirituous varnish, used chiefly for touching over the knots in wood-work previous to the priming, or first coating, with paint. It is also useful for coating over stains and other effects of dampness on walls previous to painting them.

Japan, or *Japanners' Gold Size* is a liquid used for a variety of purposes. Japan gold size is a preparation of linseed oil and litharge, and will usually dry in about half an hour. Although the name appears to connect it with processes of gilding, it is seldom used for that purpose, but rather as a liquid driers in combination with turps and flatting paint. When nearly dry, it has to a slight degree that property of tackiness which is so characteristic of oil gold size, but with very little of the brilliancy of the latter. Only on out-door work, where it is advisable to complete the gilding forthwith, for temporary work, or for sign writing, can it be recommended as a *gold size*.

Compositions prepared with japan gold size for hardening them are much used in coach painting, engine work, and, to a minor extent, in house painting and "filling up"; and in preparing "dead" black from *Ivory Black* ground in turpentine, this is also the best and safest binding liquid.

A few words must now be said about *driers*, as they are very important. Many people use them too freely, to the detriment of the paints. Of these substances there is a considerable variety, which may be used to more or less advantage, according to their chemical nature and their effect upon the colour of paint.

Red Lead is a good natural drier, but this would not do for assisting the *white* paint to oxidise. The principal drying materials for all liquids and paints are sugar of lead, sulphate of zinc, litharge or oxide of lead, white copperas, white sulphate of manganese, and white borate of manganese, of which the two last are the most expensive. Nowadays, it is not necessary to rub up our own litharge or sugar of lead, for they are offered to us in the less pure, perhaps, but far more convenient form of *liquid driers* and *patent driers* respectively.

Don't use driers which form a dark matter on the top in the keg, or such as have a brittle skin—for they dry too hard—or such as turn a livid white under water. Don't use driers which have a body or are of a dark colour. In former days, sugar of lead was ground for driers. In every painter's shop was a large muller and stone slab, upon which all the colours were ground (there were no tube colours then), and a stock job consisted in grinding sugar of lead, that and litharge being the general driers. Longer time was then allowed for paint to dry, and driers were used sparingly.

Liquid driers, such as terebine, are composed of oils or spirits which have been subjected to the action of a siccative or drying material. This action of drying is an instance of a quick way of bringing about what nature accomplishes in a longer time. Instead of losing a portion of their bulk, as is the case with water colours, oil colours, in drying, take up oxygen from the air: a process which chemistry shows is constantly going on with nearly everything on the earth's surface. It is easily seen that the slow drying of nature is the best, and that excess of driers will harden the surface of the colour too quickly, and cause the outer surface to contract and become smaller than the under surface. The tension between them causes cracking. It is purposely done to produce fancy cracking in pottery work. The glaze and colour are so made that the glaze contracts quicker than the colour in the cooling; and the result is cracks all over the ware. Such substances as Japanese gold size or varnish will make the paint brittle and produce the same effect. Drying oil or sugar of lead is the best to use. Good terebine also is a safe drier.

Every colour and varnish manufacturer now makes a terebine or liquid drier, and its drying strength is usually that of 1 oz. to the lb. of paint, under favourable conditions. Terebine combines far more satisfactorily with linseed oil for drying than does Japan gold size : a similar mixture. The latter is most useful in compounding flatting and quick-drying paints for varnishing upon.

A sample of terebine, purchased at a paint-shop and afterwards tested, was found to contain 75 per cent. of turps and 25 per cent. of a residue consisting almost entirely of boiled linseed oil, but containing also a little common resin—added, no doubt, as an adulterant. The boiled oil it contained was of a dark brown colour, and had been boiled with oxide of lead (litharge), in order to render it quicker as a drying agent. It is safe to say that terebine may be made by mixing together 25 per cent. of boiled linseed oil (treated with litharge) and 75 per cent. of turpentine : in other words, ¾ lb. of turps and ¼ lb. of oil ; but each maker may have a different formula.

Another recipe for making this useful material for painters is as follows :—Take 2 lbs. ground litharge, 2 lbs. red lead, 1 lb. sulphate of manganese, ½ lb. sugar of lead ; put all these into a pot, and mix with them four or five gills of pale Japan gold size, until the lot can be easily stirred. Then add about ½ gal. of American turpentine. Now leave the whole to stand, with occasional stirring, for a few days (not less than three), and its materials will act without heat. After the expiration of a few days, the clear resultant liquid—terebine—may be taken off, and more "turps" put on the materials, for the *second* and *third time*, with equally satisfactory results. Half proportions of these component articles may be used with equally good results.

Many samples of paraffin give what is called a fluorescence—that is, though the oil is apparently colourless, if you hold some in a test-tube against a black background (a coat-sleeve), and allow the light to be reflected from it, you will find that it has a fine delicate blue colour or bloom. Now, pure turpentine does not show a fluorescence, and by trial it has been found that 10 per cent. of paraffin oil added gave a slight fluorescence on the surface of the mixture. The only point against this test is that some samples of paraffin oil do not give a fluorescence, but there are not many of them; resin oil, the chief adulterant for turpentine, is also fluorescent, and has to be detected by its high gravity. If there is a smell of paraffin oil and fluorescence, it is certain there is paraffin present.

One of the simplest tests is to put a few drops of the turpentine on a sheet of white writing-paper. If the turpentine is pure, it will evaporate in a few minutes, leaving the paper quite clean; while if it be adulterated with paraffin oil (petroleum), it will leave a greasy mark. If the adulterant used is benzine, the greasy mark will not be so apparent, and will fade away in the course of about five minutes. Another good test for the practical painter is to shake up the turpentine in a small bottle. It is well to obtain a sample of turpentine of undoubted purity, and place this into a small bottle. Shake up the sample, and note the result; then immediately shake up the suspected turpentine, comparing the two. The bubbles in turpentine adulterated with petroleum will hold longer than those in pure material, and a blue cast will be observable if the bottle be held in a strong light. It should be added that old turpentine that has become gummy, even if pure, will leave a greasy mark on white paper, which might be taken to indicate the presence of petroleum in the test above mentioned. As, however, gum in turpentine is just as objectionable as the presence of paraffin oil, this fact does not interfere with the usefulness of the test.

CHAPTER IV.

TOOLS USED BY PAINTERS.

THE purpose of this chapter is to describe the particular kinds of tools and requisites with which the painter has to work, and to further afford some measure of advice for the guidance of purchasers. As brushes are the chief tools in a painter's outfit, they will be dealt with first.

The best bristles used in making painters' brushes are imported from Russia. The hairs of the hog and wild boar are noted for their strength and size. They grow to some nine inches long. St. Petersburg, Kamschatka, and the wilds of Siberia annually contribute a large proportion of the immense quantity used for brush making. A goodly number of their bristles are shed or rubbed off by the hogs during the summer-time, and when collected into a sufficiently large bundle, these are sent by the peasantry from all parts of the country to trade centres. France and Belgium also contribute a small proportion of bristles to the market, and Germany not only sends us the hair, but a great quantity of cheap and rubbishy vegetable fibre brushes also ; for the supply of the best and most serviceable bristles and brushes scarcely keeps pace with the growing demands and requirements of the painting and decorative trades, and hence a market is found here for the less serviceable but more showy-looking brushes which flood the trade.

The value of hogs' bristles naturally depends upon their suitability for brush making—their length, strength, elasticity, and also colour. *White* brushes are commonly preferred, not only by house-painters, but also in all descriptions of brushes, probably under the impression that adulteration is less prevalent than with grey- or black-haired brushes. Bristles are bought by weight; and the cause for the vast difference in the price and quality between two ordinary-looking paint-brushes may be inferred from the fact that the price of genuine bristles ranges from about £10 to nearly £50 per hundredweight.

The adulteration of brushes is carried on to a vast extent, and principally by the aid of American fibre and horsehair. So well are these adulterants manipulated and mixed with the bristles, that it is a difficult matter to discover them. Horsehair is more difficult to detect by examination, since the difference between that and poor bristles is but in the quality of elasticity. When fibre is mixed with the hair, a loss of "spring" in the brush is

Fig. 10.—Ordinary House Painter's Brush.

noticeable, as is also the appearance of the fibre—it is neither so smooth or finished-looking as hair. The difference observable in burning a vegetable fibre, which will leave a grey ash, and the peculiar smell attending the burning of hair or bristle, quickly decides which is under examination. But burning is no test between bristle and horsehair—here experience alone can decide.

The accompanying illustrations have been selected chiefly to show the peculiarities of each class or make of brush, without consideration of the exact size or scale. They include examples of most descriptions of brushes in ordinary use for painting and varnishing; and with all these the painter should be familiar. Fig. 10 will convey a fair idea of the appearance of an ordinary good paint-brush of the usual form. The bristles are about 6 in. long from the binding to the point, and each brush requires to be bridled—that is, tied up with string some 2 or 3 in. higher—before it is used for painting. As the brush wears down, the string binding is untied, until eventually the extra bridle is entirely dispensed with. Fig. 11 is a similar brush, but oval in shape. Fig. 12 represents a shape in which quantities of cheap brushes are made. These three kinds of brushes are usually sold in four qualities of bristle: "Lily," "Yellow Middle," "Grey," and "Black," of which the first and whitest is the best and most expensive. Good hair makes a good brush, made up in either shape, but

Fig. 11.—House Painter's ordinary Oval Brush.

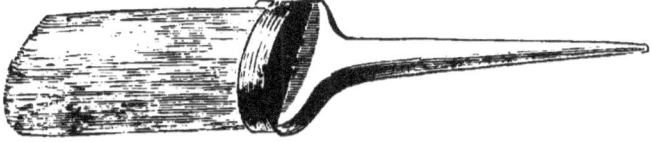

Fig. 12.—Cheap Style of Brush, with Copper Binding.

Fig. 13.—English Sash Tool.

Fig. 14.—Small Sash Tool.

Fig. 15.—German Paint Tool.

the first shape is mostly used at the first-rate decorators' shops.

Fig. 13 shows a small round-handle brush, called an English paint tool, the shape of which is never altered; the small sizes are called "sash tools"—that is, for painting the small bars of a window-sash. They all require tying up short for using in oil paint. The German paint tool (Fig. 15), both for wear and quality, compares very unfavourably; and although it can be bought for half the price of a good English tool, it is dear at that to a worker. An assortment of sash tools are illustrated in Figs. 13 to 18.

Fig. 19 represents a brush of recent date, made pur-

Fig. 16.—Long Haired Sash Tool.

Fig. 17.—Quilled Sash Tool.

Fig. 18.—Sash Tool for General Use.

Fig. 19.—Sash-Painting Tool.

Fig. 20.—Hog-hair Fitch in round Tin.

Fig. 21.—Hog-hair in flat Tin.

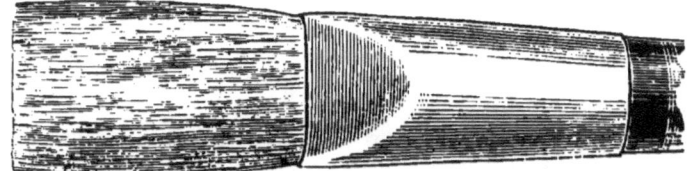

Fig. 22.—Hog-hair flat Tool.

posely for sash-painting; it is an assistance to quick and clean work, where a great number of window-panes have to be painted, but for ordinary work the string-tied sash tool will suffice. Figs. 20 and 21 are termed "fitches," consisting of short bristles bound in tin, with long wood handles. They are much used for all kinds of decorating and gilding; and nearly all painters, artistic and otherwise, find them indispensable. Fig. 23 is a somewhat similar brush, useful to gilders, scene-painters, etc., as well as to decorators.

Painters' varnish-brushes are usually old and well-

Fig. 23.—French Round Tool.

Fig. 24.—Oval Bevelled Varnish Brush.

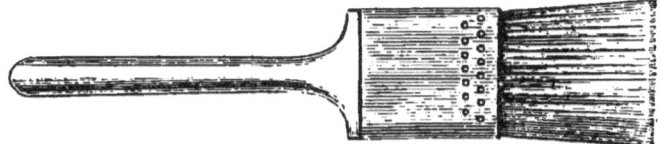

Fig. 25.—Flat Varnish Brush in Tin.

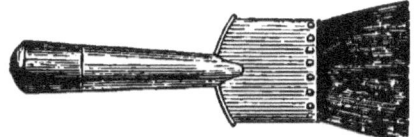

Fig. 26.—Varnishing Fitch.

tried tools that have been worn-in with painting, and these, if properly cleaned and looked after, cannot be improved upon for professional use. Figs. 24, 25, and 26 represent brushes specially made for varnishing; the first, shown edgewise, it will be noticed, is made to the shape of a partly-worn paint-brush. Fig. 25 is a shape occasionally used by the operative house painter; certainly not by reason of its suitability. This and Fig. 26 can be used to advantage only on the finest work, and on broad flat surfaces.

Clean and good work cannot be done without dusting-brushes. Fig. 27 shows the best shape, the pointed handle is useful to remove dirt from corners. Somewhat similar in shape to Fig. 10, on p. 60, it is rather larger, and the bristles are much longer and spreading, so that dust and dirt can be brushed out of any crevice and corner with ease. Brushes like Fig. 12, made only for

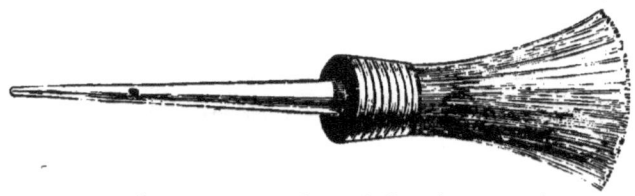

Fig. 27.—House Painters' Dusting Brush.

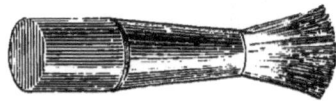

Fig. 28.—Stencil Tool.

Fig. 29.—Lining Fitch in flat Handle.

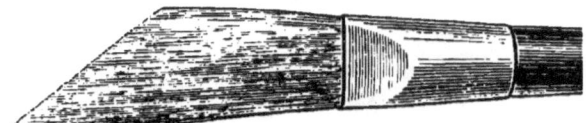

Fig. 30.—Hog-hair Lining Fitch.

painting, are sometimes used for dusting, and when by such unfair usage the hairs come out, the maker is often blamed without reason.

Fig. 28, a stencil-brush, and Figs. 29 and 30, fitches, are brushes more used by decorators than by painters. The former is for stencilling, and the latter for running lines with the aid of a bevelled straight-edge. The prices of these, like all brushes, depend upon the size.

Fig. 31 shows a section of the straight-edge used to guide a lining fitch. A is the side laid against the surface, the fitch is guided by the edge c, and the space B prevents paint spreading.

Figs. 32 to 36 show a variety of larger brushes specially made for distemper painting and preparation.

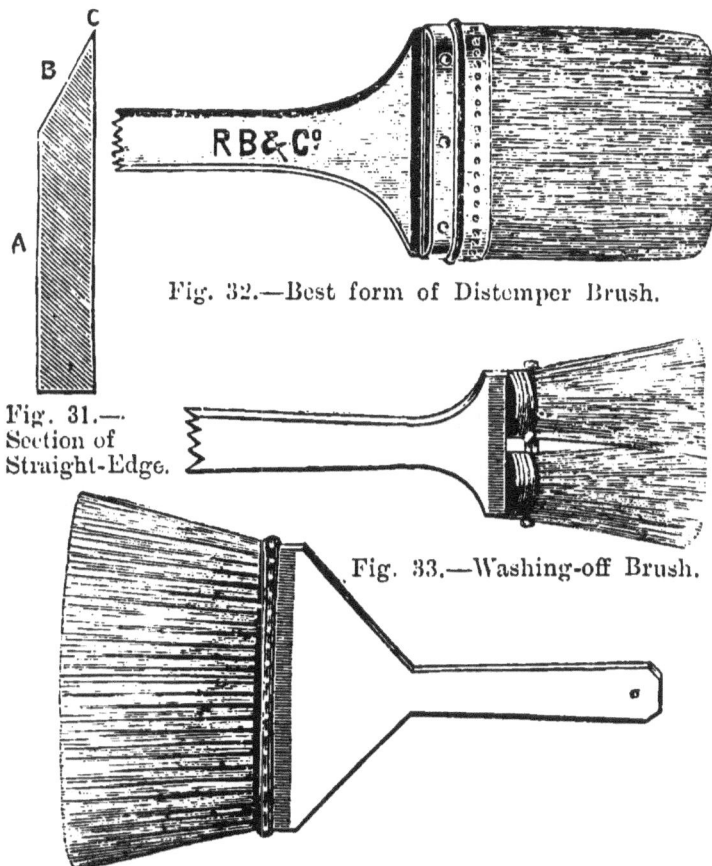

Fig. 31.—Section of Straight-Edge.

Fig. 32.—Best form of Distemper Brush.

Fig. 33.—Washing-off Brush.

Fig. 34.—Paddle Distemper Brush on Nailed Stock.

Fig. 32 is the distemper-brush, such as is used by the leading decorators for the best kind of work. This form of brush is fitted with a strong brass band. The best and finest are made with yellow and grey bristles, which are about 6 in. long. These brushes are without doubt the most suitable size and shape for spreading properly prepared "jellied" distemper.

Fig. 35.—Scotch Distemper Brush.   Fig. 36.—Pasting Brush.

Fig. 37.—Limer, used with a Long Handle.

Fig. 33 represents a useful brush, made of black hair and fibre, for washing off old distemper from ceilings and walls. Fig. 34 shows the distemper-brush very general in the West of England and other provincial parts, where it is commonly known as a "paddle" brush. Nothing but a wash can be spread with them. Its broad thin shape tells plainly how little jellied distemper is understood and used in parts where the "paddle" is called for. They are always made with grey or black hair. Fig. 35 is a good shape, but rather too

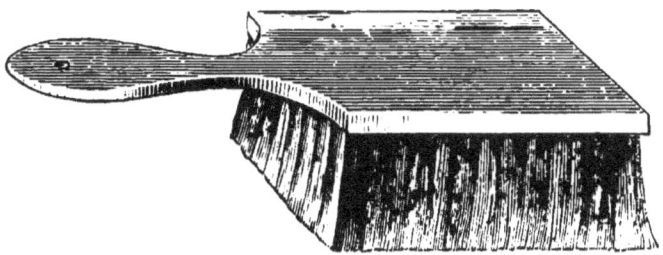

Fig. 38.—Stippler.

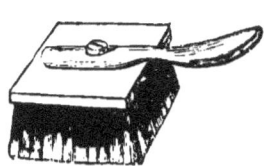

Fig. 39.—Stippler with Reversible Handle.

Fig. 40.—Stippler with Bridge Handle.

heavy and clumsy for best work. The five kinds just described are always made with handles, as shown.

Fig. 37 is made for use with a long handle; otherwise, it corresponds closely with Fig. 33. In some parts of the country this "limer" is the principal ceiling-brush used. A practised hand can get over a great quantity of sizing and distemper washing with one, and save erecting the scaffold also. Limers of the best kind are as expensive as distemper brushes. Fig. 36 represents a good pasting-brush, and useful for distemper work also.

Stipplers are the most costly of painters' brushes. They are used for obliterating the brush markings, in "flatting" and other processes, by a beating action, executed evenly and carefully after the paint is applied and roughly distributed. They require careful attention to keep in order, and should directly after use be washed with plenty of soap and warm water, without wetting the "stock" or wood. When all the paint is removed, rinse in cold water, and accelerate the drying by beating on a dry cloth or wash-leather. Fig. 38 shows one with handle at end; they are also made

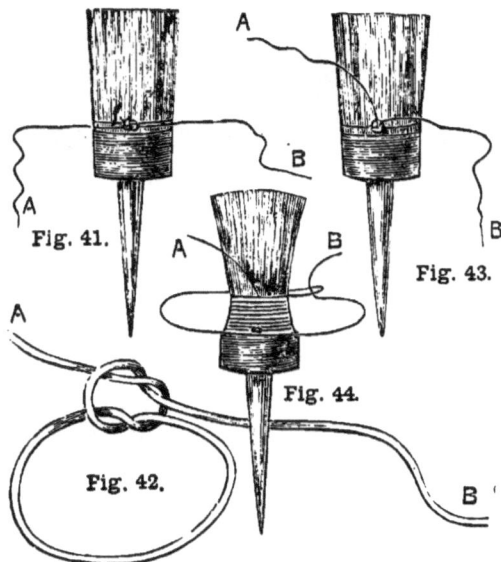

Figs. 41 to 44.—How to Tie a Paint Brush.

with handles on the back and reversible handles. Fig. 39 has a reversible handle; Fig. 40 has a bridge handle. They are used for distributing paint or vehicles in a perfectly regular manner, and for taking out paint-brush streaks. In use, the paint is first spread—a good coat—and then the work is at once stippled with the ends of bristles until a regular surface of a granular nature is obtained.

Many people who need a paint-brush find that it is too long and limp to work well. It needs tying.

This is a difficulty to the inexperienced; and here is a method of tying a brush.

First tie a piece of stout twine (that used for Macramé work will do well) round the brush, leaving 6 in. or 7 in. at one end (marked A in the sketch). Fig. 41 shows the first tie. Fig. 42 shows the form of knot used. The end A should be made to lie along the hair of the brush, Fig. 43, and the string should be coiled round it and the hair of the brush as many times as necessary. When enough has been wound around, Fig. 44, the cord marked B may be bent back, drawn close, and a half-knot made opposite the first knot. Both cords may now be fixed with small tacks to the stock or the handle of the

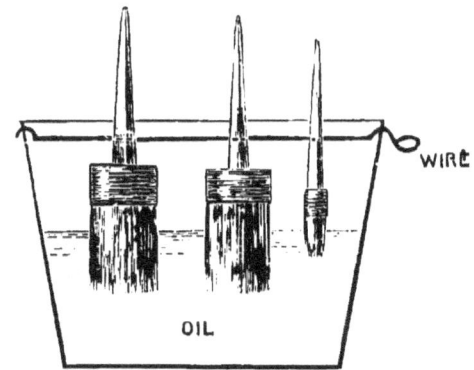

Fig. 45.—Preserving Paint Brushes.

brush, and the superfluous string cut off. The string need not be bound very tightly, for either paint or water will make it sufficiently tight for the purpose for which it is intended. From time to time, part of the string can be removed as the bristles wear away.

Paint-brushes naturally get hard and useless if left exposed to the air with paint in the bristles, since the very property that causes the paint to dry causes this hardening. If the brushes are small and used very seldom, they should have the paint rinsed out with a little turpentine or petroleum, then they should be carefully washed clean with soap in warm water, well rinsed in cold water, and then set aside to dry gradually. Soda ruins the bristles, and hot water dissolves the cement that holds the bristles to the handles ; so do not use either. Brushes used so often that they cannot be washed between whiles, should have the paint well scraped out, and the brush then stood in a vessel with sufficient water to cover the bristles ; but not more than that, since the string binding the brush gets rotted. Varnish brushes must be served exactly as those used for paint, so far as washing goes ; but if they are large brushes, and often required, they must be carefully stood in a vessel

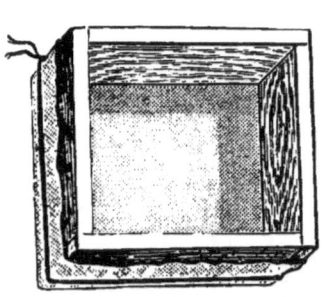

Fig. 46.—Paint Straining Sieve.

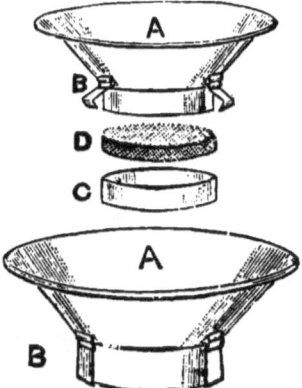

Fig. 47.—Patent Paint Strainer.

containing raw linseed oil instead of water, as with paint-brushes. Each time the brush is required and done with, scrape water, paint, and oil out of it.

The accompanying illustration (Fig. 45) shows a good method of preserving brushes. Clean out the brushes well, and make a hole in the handles to let the wire pass through, and then let them hang from the wire without touching the bottom ; let them dip in linseed oil.

Fig. 45 shows an easily-made sieve for straining paints. It is made of four strips of wood about 12 in. long, 4 in. wide, and ½ in. thick, nailed together to form a frame. A piece of coarse canvas tacked or tied to the frame forms the strainer.

Fig. 47 illustrates a recently-introduced improvement in paint strainers, which ought to find favour among painters and colourmen. This consists in making the strainer in such a form that the copper wire gauze which is used as a strainer may be removed, and a fresh piece put on in a very short space of time, thus saving the body of the strainer, and rendering it still useful when the wire gauze has been worn out. The illustration, Fig. 47, shows the body of the strainer, A, at top, fitted with the clips, B. The wire gauze, D, fits over the lower

Fig. 48.—Chisel-pointed Stopping Knife.

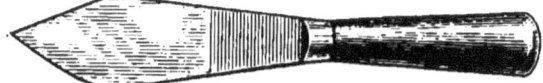

Fig. 49.—Stopping Knife.

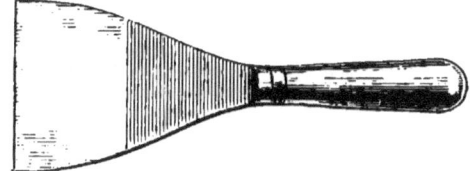

Fig. 50.—Chisel or Broad Knife.

part of the strainer, and is held in place by what is called the compression band, C, over which the clips, B, fit down, holding the different parts tightly together. In the lower part of the illustration the strainer is shown with the gauze and band on, and the clips closed down. The strainer costs 2s., and the gauzes, which are made in three sizes, are sold at 5d. per piece.

Five of the knives most used by the house painter are shown. Fig. 48 represents a chisel knife; or it may be termed a stopping knife with chisel point. Fig. 49 shows the most useful shape of stopping knife, with which holes and indentations of wood-work, etc., are filled with putty. Fig. 50 is the "chisel knife" proper, but as often termed the broad knife; this is used for stripping and scraping old walls, filling up wood-work, stopping plaster walls, etc., and is a very useful tool. Fig. 51 is a knife having a thin steel blade; it is used for mixing paints on a slab. Fig. 52 and Fig. 53 are more properly glaziers' knives than house painters'; the first is the putty knife, indispensable for glazing sashes, and the latter the hacking knife, for use with a hammer for chipping out the old hard putty previous to re-glazing.

A portable balcony, used when painting windows

Fig. 51.—Palette Knife.

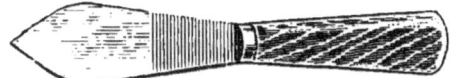

Fig. 52.—Glazier's Putty Knife.

Fig. 53.—Glazier's Hacking Knife.

outside, is shown in the illustrations on page 73. Fig. 54 is a side elevation, and Fig. 55 a perspective sketch of a contrivance used by painters when painting and cleaning the outsides of windows. It is used in this way:—The lower sash is raised, and the bracketed portion is put outside, and dropped down until the board rests on the sash-bead on the sill of window. The abutment piece, c, is then pulled tightly against the outside of wall, and the pins, A, are put through two of the most convenient of the holes, marked B. That will allow of the pins pinching against the nosing of window board inside the room. A piece of wood or soft cloth should be first put over the window board, to prevent damage; sometimes it is necessary to pack out between the nosing and the pins, A. The holes, B, should be made quite square and true, so that the pins fit tightly in and will not wobble. Sometimes the holes are first made in

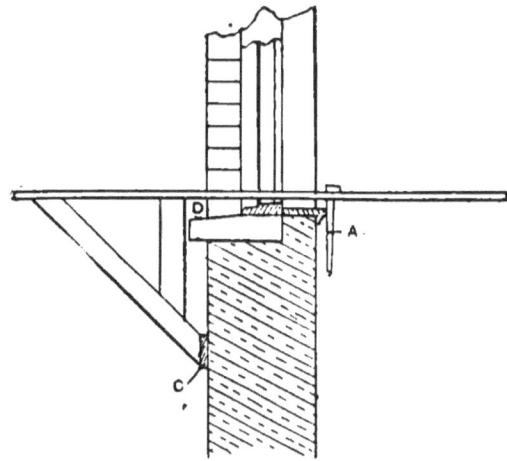

Fig. 54.—Portable Balcony in position for use.

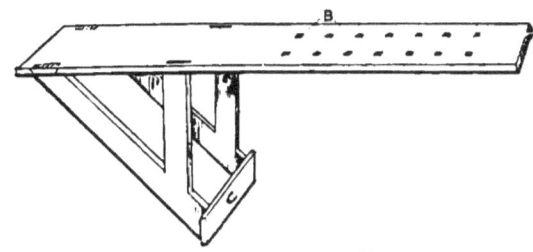

Fig. 55.—Perspective Sketch of Portable Balcony.

strips of iron plate, and then screwed on top and bottom of the board, and the holes through the wood made between the holes in the iron. This prevents the wood wearing, and so allowing the pins to become loose. A piece of packing should be put on the window-sill outside, at D. Although this arrangement is much used, it does not appear so safe as it ought to be.

CHAPTER V.

HOW TO MIX OIL PAINTS.

To set down exactly the proportions of different pigments necessary for producing any desired tint or colour may, at first sight, appear an easy task. For instance: it may be said, "Mix together three parts of lead, two of black, and one of yellow," but the practical information given is small. Apart from the fact that there is a great number of different browns, ideas vary considerably as to what is a brown; and this applies to every other colour. If a dozen practical house painters were asked to mix a maroon paint, it is almost certain that no two of them would be exactly alike, even though compounded from the same materials. When opinions differ so widely as to the exact tint or shade of a named colour, to give proportions of materials with exactness in the above-mentioned formula has but indefinite value, because the kind of red is not mentioned; nor, indeed, is the kind of yellow, nor of black.

Another and even more important reason makes it impossible to give exact proportions; and this is owing to the strength and quality of paints of different manufacture differing so largely. The pigments used by one maker may be strictly pure, while those used by another may contain fifty per cent. of adulterant, and for that reason be only of half the full tinting strength; or they may be pure, and yet be deficient in tinting strength. Hence it will be seen that even with a sample colour to work to, the results would differ unless materials were used of exactly the same quality in each case.

Although it is not possible to give proportions of materials in figures, it is possible to give some idea of the amount of each colour that should be used; and in making out the list which follows, the proportions in each case are indicated as closely as it is safe to go. It is supposed that pigments of first quality are used ; and the reader must be warned that if inferior pigments are employed the tints produced by the admixture of them will always be more or less unsatisfactory, having, as a rule, a muddy cast that is very objectionable.

A word may be said as to the names of colours used in the following list :—It would be an easy matter to make the list ten times longer than it is by including all the names of colours that are used in the arts, especially those employed by the manufacturers of textiles. Turning, for instance, to a list of new colours for ladies' dresses, we find "liseron," a pink having a violet tinge ; "venus," a flesh pink ; "iris," a pale flesh shade ; "gluten," a deep cream ; "australien," a deep orange ; "skobeleff," a bright green ; "aloes," a medium grey-green ; and many others. Then there are a thousand and one colours bearing even more fanciful names, such as "elephant's breath," "crushed strawberry" (now a well-defined colour among linen-drapers), "maiden's tears," etc. ; in fact, it is puzzling to know the extent to which such names will go.

And names of pigments are not always synonymous with the colours. Dutch pink is yellow; verditer is blue ; lake is not purple-blue always, but sometimes green, yellow, brown, etc.; or it may be found as a pigment colour, with a chalk base, or body, for fugitive colours.

Before proceeding to describe the actual method of mixing, a few general remarks on colours may be given. White lead is used for the base of paints, because that pigment possesses greater covering properties—or body, as it is technically termed—than any other. Zinc white may be used for a base under certain conditions, and colour mixed with it will not be so likely to fade as when mixed with lead. The tendency of zinc white, however, to chip and crack renders the addition of lead necessary in most cases. When practicable, the natural earth pigments should be used for tinting purposes in preference to those which are manufactured. Raw umbers, raw siennas, etc., will be found to last longer than burnt umbers and burnt siennas. As a rule, burnt umber should not be used for outside painting, but the required shade should be obtained by mixing lamp-black and an oxide colour, such as Venetian red.

Common colours include lamp-black, red lead, white lead, Venetian red, umbers, and all other common ochres, such as greys, buffs, stones, etc. Superior or ornamental colours include bright yellows, warm tints, blues, mineral greens, etc. Some colours—such as verditer, pea greens, rich reds, pinks, and bright blues—are charged at a higher rate still as delicate tints.

In compounding pigments for painting, there is yet a further matter requiring some little consideration by the worker. All blue pigments are not chemically suitable for mixture with yellows or reds, nor all yellows with reds—in fact, a knowledge of the chemical source and affinities of pigments is almost a necessity to the painter and decorator. As the most brief and simple way of aiding the student, it will be well to mention those ordinary pigments which it is usually advisable *not* to mix together.

For mixing with oil colour paints, chrome is an undesirable pigment, and it is particularly to be avoided when compounding *greens* from *Prussian* or *Antwerp* blues, which latter colours it would eventually destroy. In such an instance, for common use the best substitute for the chrome would be bright *yellow ochre*, or, as it is often labelled, yellow paint. *Raw sienna* can also be used with the above blue pigments without much detriment to either. In any case where a bright *mixed* green is absolutely necessary, the lemon chrome can be used in conjunction with good *ultramarine* blue or *indigo*.

In compounding the secondary colour of *purple* from blues and reds, there is less danger of trouble arising. For oil painting, the best and purest are obtained by mixing ultramarine with *madder lake* (which is a beautiful crimson and transparent permanent pigment), while lakes derived from cochineal are unstable, or ultramarine and vermilion will answer. Prussian blue and vermilion give very deep purple, which may be lighted up with white. For common purposes, the cheap purple brown is most useful, if required full in strength; but if lighter and pure tints are wanted in oil or distemper, ultramarine blue and vermilion, or, for cheapness, Venetian red, is necessary. Prussian blue in water would *not* suit so well, but indigo could be used if cost is not a consideration.

The remaining secondary, *orange*, is not a colour very much called for. In *orange chrome* or *orange red* we have a bright opaque pigment, but otherwise, like all the chromes, not a commendable article. *Burnt sienna* is a very opposite pigment in both nature and source. It is semi-transparent, reliable, and permanent, and—what also the practical student must always bear in mind—it is, when of good quality, a remarkably strong stainer, like Prussian blue in this respect. In compounding orange colour, the reds and ochres already mentioned are usually bright enough; yellow ochre and Venetian red, or raw and burnt sienna together, give us, with white lead, a good and serviceable variety of permanent orange and salmon tints.

The compounding of the third division of material colours, the tertiary, from either of the two secondaries, is a subject that need scarcely here be dealt with. The student who works at this subject practically will soon find, from the foregoing and subsequent remarks, those secondary pigments of orange and green which produce the tertiary *citrine*, whether bright or sombre, such as occasion requires. Of the remaining tertiaries, *russet* and *olive*, prepared from the secondaries purple and orange, purple and green, respectively, we have a good supply in the form of simple pigments. Notwithstanding, therefore, the necessity and advantage of the worker being able to obtain any colour by the admixture of the three primaries, it is always most economical to use a simple article of the desired colour when it is to be had.

In the actual mixing of paints, it must not be thought that there is any one way that is exactly right while all other methods are exactly wrong. Every painter has his own peculiar way. In nearly all cases, the simplest plan is to use pigments ground in oil instead of dry powders. With a pallet knife break up the lead rather stiff, adding a little oil. Thin down each paint until it is rather stiffer than the whole will be when ready for actual application; or if dry pigments be used, add a little oil, and thoroughly mix. The lead, zinc, or other base being ready, add some pigment, and well stir. If several pigments are required to produce the tint, be sure to add only one at a time, and take great care that each is *thoroughly* mixed before the next one is added. As a further precaution, it is well not to add the pigment all at once, but to do so a little at a time. When it is certain that a thorough admixture has been effected, the next pigment may be added a little at a time. It is well to remember that some pigments, such as Prussian blue, are very strong, and the addition of too much will spoil the job. It is easy to add a little more, while it is impossible to take any out. A little precaution in this respect will save much trouble; and although it takes longer to mix a batch of paint, it is the much safer plan. Of course, a practical man who is used to frequently mixing paints can add the necessary amount of colours without taking these precautions.

Having mixed the paint, add as much driers as may be necessary, taking care not to use too much. Then the paint should be strained through a fine wire strainer. It is well to mix up enough of the paint in one batch to do the whole of the job in hand, so that there may be no trouble or waste of time in matching tints. Paint mixed in cold weather is very likely to give unsatisfactory results, because the oil will stiffen and be more difficult to form into a perfect admixture. To remedy this, a gallon or so of the oil should be heated, and this poured in will warm up the paint, and prevent it "pulling" when applied, and so avoid the unnecessary force required to draw the brush along.

In preparing oil paint, the first question to be considered is the nature of the surface to be painted, whether of wood, stone, or metal, and to what degree it is absorbent; second to this must be remembered the conditions and position of the work, such as refer to expense, durability, and drying qualities; and lastly, to bear in mind the all-important matter of appearance and colour, whether the paint is for the first or last coat. We will therefore proceed to an imaginary mixing of paint for wood, stone, and metal, bringing in a lesson on their application to the walls and wood-work of a building.

The quantities of driers, oil, and turpentine required to bring 1 cwt. of white lead to the consistency of paint is a matter that must be varied according to the conditions of the work it is required for. In summer-time, 1 lb. of good driers to 14 of white lead is ample for out-door purposes; in winter-time, 1 in 10 would be best. The quantity of oils required would be about 1½ gallons for the cwt. of lead. The proportions of linseed oil and oil of turpentine it is advisable to use depends entirely upon the purpose we intend it for. With reference to the question of boiled or unboiled oil, it should be remembered that both oils are glossy when applied in sufficient quantity; boiled linseed oil has more body, and is more brilliant than raw linseed oil; raw linseed oil is lighter in colour, and is not so liable to blister as boiled linseed oil; boiled linseed oil dries quicker than raw linseed oil.

To mix 1 lb. of ordinary oil paint, take about 8 ozs. of pigment the desired colour: thus, white lead for white, light greys, pinks, cream, etc.; Venetian red or vermilion for red; and so on, according to the price and colour desired. Add to this about 2 ozs. of patent paste or liquid driers; then make up to 1 lb. with either linseed oil alone or oil and turpentine in equal parts. Remember, the more oil the more driers is advisable, but never less than 1 part driers in 8 or 10 of entire bulk. If only casual pounds of paint are wanted, that sold ready mixed, at prices from 3½d. to 5d. per lb., according to district and maker, would be cheapest, and should do for common inside work. A single pound could not be made so cheaply, and some of the colours sold—bright red, for instance—could not be made at twice the figure. If varnished, they stand a lot of wear.

To make French grey paint.—The ingredients for making about 40 lbs. of best glossy paint for indoors, tinted to a French grey colour, would be, say, ¼ cwt. (28 lbs.) *genuine* white lead, 3 lbs. best patent driers, about ½ gallon raw linseed oil, and 1 quart turpentine. Mix up the lead and driers with a broad stick to the consistency of a thick paste, using linseed oil. If all is to be tinted one colour, for French grey add a little ultramarine blue and either a little Venetian red or common black. If a warm grey is wanted, add the red; if a cool metallic tint, add the black. The ultramarine can only be bought in powder; well mix this with a little oil before adding it to the paint; the other colours can easily be obtained ready ground in oil. Respecting the economical aspect of ready-mixed *v.* best paint, it cannot be expected that the former, sold as low as 3½d. per lb. in some parts, can be equal in value to the best white lead paint, especially as the *genuine* white lead may cost 4d. per lb. The blue powder will probably cost about 2s. 6d. per lb., and at least ½ lb. will be required. The liquids lower the average cost per lb. when the quantity is all made ready for use; but when one considers the time required for making the paint, matching a particular colour, and then straining the paint through muslin or a very fine sieve, the price usually asked for such best paint—viz., 6d. per lb.—is but fair value. For first coating on new plaster, one can use nearly all linseed oil and a little driers—very little lead. This will stop the suction of the plaster. As a rule, new plaster requires four coats to get a good surface.

The following alphabetical list of colours, with proportions of ingredients, will be found useful :—

Amaranth.—This is a bright brown. It is made by mixing together light Tuscan red and vermilion, with the addition of a small quantity of ultramarine blue.

Amber Brown.—Use orange chrome yellow, burnt sienna, burnt umber, and lamp-black, and add white until the desired shade is produced.

Antique Bronze.—Mix together orange chrome yellow and ivory black.

Apple Green.—Use light chrome green, white lead, and orange chrome yellow.

Ashes of Roses.—Mix together light Tuscan red and lamp-black.

Azure.—This is a beautiful tone of blue, that may be best described as a dark shade of sky blue. Take white as a base, and add Prussian blue until the requisite shade is obtained.

Bismarck Brown.—This colour may be bought ready for use, and it may be lightened if necessary. To imitate it, mix burnt sienna, orange chrome yellow, and burnt umber, and lighten up with white lead.

Bottle Green.—Take Prussian blue, and add a small quantity of lamp-black and a little lemon chrome yellow. The colour will be principally made up of the blue, the black and yellow producing the requisite greenish cast.

Brass.—Add medium chrome yellow, French ochre, and a little umber to white as a base.

Brick Colour.—By brick colour is generally meant a slightly yellowish-red, sometimes termed brick red. It may be produced by adding Venetian red and white to yellow ochre. Two parts of ochre, one of red, and one of white give some idea of the proportions to use, but less white may be often used with advantage.

Bronze Green.—This is a mixture of chrome green, black, and umber. If very dark chrome green is used, very little, if any, of the umber will be required. The black may be either lamp or ivory black. The proportions of the colours will, of course, depend upon the exact shade required : five parts of medium chrome green, one part of lamp-black, and one part of umber, all of good quality, will give an excellent bronze green of about a medium degree of intensity.

Brown.—There are many different shades of brown, varying from very light to very dark. They may all be produced by using Venetian red as a base, and adding lamp-black and yellow ochre. Three parts of red, two of black, and one of yellow ochre give a medium rich brown, and other shades may be produced by using more or less of the black and yellow. A little white may be added when it is desired to give the brown a drabbish cast.

Brown Stone.—Mix orange chrome yellow, dark Tuscan red, and lamp-black. Add white lead until the desired tint is obtained.

Buff.—Light or dark buffs are made by taking white as the base, and adding French ochre. If a very dark buff is required, a very little Venetian red may be added; but, as a rule, the French ochre will be sufficient. Chrome yellow and white, tinged with Venetian red, may also be used.

Buttercup Yellow.—This colour is produced simply by mixing together lemon chrome yellow and white lead.

Canary.—This is simply a very light but bright yellow. Add lemon chrome yellow to white until the desired shade is obtained. If an average chrome is used, the proportions will be about three parts of yellow to five of white.

Carnation.—This beautiful red is made by adding carmine to pure vermilion, lightening up with zinc white, if necessary. It need hardly be added that to obtain the requisite purity and intensity of carnation, only the best vermilion and carmine must be used.

Cerulean.—This is obtained by lightening up ultramarine blue with white.

Chestnut.—This colour is generally accepted as that of the skin of the chestnut—a rich brown. It is made from Venetian red as a base, with the addition thereto of medium chrome yellow, yellow ochre, and lamp-black, in about equal proportions.

Chocolate.—A very rich chocolate colour may be obtained by adding carmine to burnt umber. A less brilliant colour will be produced by using lake instead of the carmine. If a chocolate of a more brownish cast is required, make a brown by mixing Indian red and lamp-black, and lighten up with yellow ochre, or mix Spanish brown, Venetian red, and vegetable black.

Citrine.—Mix together with lead, orange chrome yellow and lamp-black.

Citron.—This is a rich and dark green, that takes its name from the citron fruit. It is made by adding Prussian blue, chrome yellow, and white to Venetian red. If a very strong colour is required, the white may be omitted.

Claret.—This colour may be obtained by mixing Venetian red and black, but by far the richest colour is obtained as follows:—Mix together ultramarine and carmine, then add vermilion, and tone down with a very little black—ivory black is best.

Clay Drabs.—These colours vary a good deal in intensity. Take white as a base, and add raw umber and raw sienna, with a very little medium chrome yellow.

Cobalt.—There is a regular blue that is sold as cobalt, and that may be used exactly as purchased; or it may be lightened up somewhat with white, if required. Cobalt cannot be successfully imitated by mixing other blues.

Copper.—To produce this colour in its full richness, only first-class materials should be employed. Six parts of Venetian red, three of medium chrome yellow, and two of lamp-black will give satisfactory results; but less of the black will frequently have to be used, especially when the red and yellow are of second-grade quality.

Cream.—Add French ochre to white. Only a little ochre will be required; if more is used, the colour would more properly be termed a buff. Chrome yellow and Venetian red added to white will also give a buff.

Crimson.—This colour may be produced by using the dark shades of scarlet reds or dark English vermilion, adding a little carmine. A richer result will be obtained if the carmine is used to glaze with.

Dove.—Lamp-black and ultramarine blue mixed with white, and tinted up with a little Indian red, will give a dove colour.

Drab.—Add to a base of white, raw or burnt umber and a little Venetian red.

Dregs of Wine.—Mix together dark Tuscan red and lamp-black, and add a little white lead.

Ecru.—This colour is intended to show the tint of raw flax or hempen fabrics, and may be produced by mixing together white lead, French ochre, burnt sienna, and lamp-black.

Electric Blue.—Ultramarine blue and white lead, to which add a little raw sienna.

Emerald Green.—A very good imitation may be obtained by using the lightest shade of chrome green.

Fawn.—Eight parts of white, two of medium chrome yellow, one of Venetian red, and one of burnt umber, all of good quality, mixed together, make a good fawn colour.

Flesh.—Use white for the base, and add yellow ochre, Venetian red, and medium chrome yellow. Use about three parts of white lead to two parts of all the colours put together, and use a little more red than of the ochre and yellow.

French Grey.—This is often made by simply adding ivory black to white; but a very small quantity of carmine and ultramarine—just enough to give a tinge— will be found to produce the truest French grey.

French Red.—The colour known by this name is made by lightening up Indian red with vermilion and glazing with carmine.

Gazelle.—Mix dark Tuscan red, Venetian red, and lamp-black; lighten up with white lead.

Gold.—Tint white with medium chrome yellow, and add a little French ochre and just a touch of vermilion;

or burnt sienna may be used instead of the ochre and vermilion.

Golden Brown.—Use French ochre, orange chrome yellow, and lamp-black, and lighten up with white lead.

Grass Green.—Three parts of lemon chrome yellow and one of Prussian blue will give a green that may be termed grass green; but to get the true grass green, use extra light chrome green just as it comes from the can. On very high-class work this green may be glazed over with Paris green, when a very handsome effect will be obtained.

Green.—There are so many shades of green that it is thought best to give the mixing of each under its distinguishing title, such as olive green, bottle green, etc.

Grey Green.—Mix together white lead, ultramarine blue, lemon chrome yellow, and lamp-black.

Greys.—Greys vary in intensity from very light to very dark. They are made simply by mixing white and lamp-black. Eight parts of white and two of black give a medium grey. They also vary considerably in the hue, which ranges from blue to brown. A little indigo added to white gives a grey of a blue hue, and light red and Prussian blue with white, a brownish hue.

Hay Colour.—Mix white lead, orange chrome yellow, light chrome green, and Tuscan or Indian red.

Jonquil.—This is a bright yellow, and the name is derived from the flower jonquil. To produce it, add a little pure vermilion to medium chrome yellow, and add this to white as a base.

Lavender.—Take white as a base, and add ivory black and a little carmine and ultramarine.

Lead Colour.—Add lamp-black and Prussian blue to white. Eight parts of white, one of black, and one of blue make an average lead colour; but some painters omit the blue or use very little, and use about one-and-a-half parts of lamp-black. Other painters prefer to use indigo.

Leaf Bud.—Mix white lead, orange chrome yellow, and light chrome green.

Leather.—This colour is made by taking French ochre as a base, and adding Venetian red and burnt umber. The latter should only be added when a warm tone is required.

Lemon.—A perfect lemon colour is first-class lemon chrome yellow, but white may be added if necessary.

Light Buff.—Add French ochre to white. Only comparatively little ochre will be required for a light buff.

Light Grey.—This is produced simply by adding lamp-black to white.

Light Oak.—Use white as a base, and add French ochre and Venetian red. Five parts of white, two of ochre, and one of red make a colour of average intensity; but ideas as to the colour of oak vary much.

Lilac.—Use white as a base, and add dark Indian red and Prussian blue in the proportion of three of the former to two of the latter. Violet lightened up with white also gives a lilac.

London Smoke.—Use yellow ochre, ultramarine blue, and lamp-black, and lighten up with white lead.

Magenta.—Mix together carmine and vermilion, and add a very little ultramarine blue.

Maroon.—Add to carmine ivory black and a small portion of orange chrome yellow. A little dark Tuscan red may also be added, if wished.

Mastic.—Use French ochre, Venetian red, and white lead, in the proportions required, and add a trifle of lamp-black.

Mauve.—Add to yellow ochre ivory or lamp-black, Venetian red, and a little white lead.

Medium Grey.—Eight parts of white and two of lamp-black make a medium grey.

Mouse.—Use white as a base, and add lamp-black and a very little burnt umber and Venetian red.

Myrtle.—Mix together dark chrome green and ultramarine, and lighten up with a little white lead.

Oak.—See light oak and dark oak.

Old Gold.—Add to white as a base medium chrome yellow, French ochre, and a little umber.

Olive.—Mix together eight parts of lemon chrome yellow, one part of lamp-black, and one part of Prussian blue. Ochre may be used instead of yellow, or both yellow and ochre together.

Olive Brown.—Mix three parts of burnt umber with one part of lemon yellow. This will give an average olive brown. A more or less intense colour can be obtained by varying the proportions of the colours.

Orange.—This colour may be made from chrome yellow.

Pea Green.—This colour is obtained simply by adding medium chrome green to white as a base. Five parts of white to one of green give an average pea green.

Peach Blossom.—White toned up with first-class Indian red will give a fine peach-blossom colour, but eight parts of white, one of Tuscan red, one of Prussian blue, and one of medium chrome yellow will give a fair substitute. Indian red, vermilion, purple brown, and white may also be used.

Peacock Blue.—Add cobalt blue to white, with a very little Chinese blue. Another way to produce the same colour is to mix very light chrome green with white lead and ultramarine blue.

Pearl.—This colour may be described as a very light French grey. It is produced by adding ivory black to white, with a faint tinge of ultramarine and carmine.

Pink.—A pink may be made by adding almost any red or lake to white—the brighter the red, the richer the pink. The richest pink is made by adding carmine to white.

Plum.—Mix together ultramarine blue and carmine; add a little ivory black and a very little white. This makes a very rich plum. More white may be used and the black omitted.

Pompeian Red.—There is a good deal of difference of opinion as to the best method of producing this colour, but vermilion, burnt sienna, and umber, lightened with ochre, may be relied upon for giving good results. A little vermilion added to Venetian red will also be found to give a good rich tone.

Portland Stone.—Add raw umber to yellow ochre, lightening up with white until the requisite tone is obtained. Three parts of yellow ochre, three parts of raw umber, and one of white will produce a somewhat dark Portland stone colour, but more of the ochre and less of umber give a colour that comes nearest to the popular idea of this colour.

Primrose.—Add to white lead as much chrome yellow as may be necessary to produce the desired intensity of colour.

Purple.—Add Indian red to white; or it may be obtained in the same manner as described for lilac, but with a larger proportion of blue.

Purple Brown.—This colour is made by mixing a dark shade of Indian red with lamp-black and ultramarine blue. The tint produced is usually too dark for practical use, and it may be lightened up with white lead as may be desired.

Quaker Drab.—Take white lead, lamp-black, burnt sienna, and French ochre, and mix together.

Robin's Egg.—This colour is produced by adding ultramarine to white, with a little light chrome green.

Rose.—Add carmine to zinc white. The purity of the white of the zinc gives a very perfect rose colour.

Russet.—Mix together raw umber, medium chrome green, and white with a little orange chrome yellow. A simpler plan is to use white lead and orange chrome yellow with a little lamp-black.

Russian Grey.—Mix together white lead, lamp-black, ultramarine blue, and pale Indian red.

Salmon.—French ochre, burnt umber, and Venetian red, added to white as a base, will produce this colour; or white lead, burnt sienna, French ochre, and a small quantity of vermilion may be used.

Scarlet.—Use pale vermilion or the various scarlet reds that are on the market.

Shrimp Pink.—Mix white lead, Venetian red, and burnt sienna, and add a little vermilion.

Silver.—Add a little indigo to white lead, with a very little black.

Sky Blue.—This may be produced by simply adding first-class Prussian blue to white.

Slate.—This colour may be obtained in the richest hue (if such it can be called) by mixing white lead, ultramarine blue, raw umber, with a small quantity of lamp-black.

Snuff Colour.—Add burnt umber to yellow ochre, and tinge with very little Venetian red; or mix together four parts of medium chrome and two of burnt umber.

Spruce Yellow.—Mix together French ochre and white lead, and add a very little Venetian red.

Stone Colour.—Mix together five parts of white, two of medium chrome yellow, and one of burnt umber. This will give a medium yellow drab; lighter or darker shades in great variety may be obtained by adding more or less of the yellow and umber.

Straw.—Add white, Venetian red, and French ochre to medium chrome yellow as a base.

Tan.—This colour is simply made by mixing white lead and burnt sienna, and adding a very little lamp-black.

Terra-cotta.—Add Venetian red and white to French ochre as a base; or mix burnt umber and orange chrome yellow, lightening up with white, as may be necessary.

Turquoise Blue.—Add to white lead, cobalt blue and Paris green, or a little light chrome green.

Violet.—Add pale Indian red to white in small proportions. A mixture of white, Prussian blue, black, and vermilion will also give a violet.

Willow Green.—Add medium chrome green to white, and add a little ivory black or burnt umber; or add five parts of white to two of verdigris.

Wine Colour.—Mix together carmine and vermilion, and add ultramarine and a very little ivory black.

Yellow Bronze.—Mix together a medium shade of chrome yellow, French ochre, and a very little burnt umber.

Yellow Lake.—Add Naples yellow and scarlet lake to equal parts of umber and white. Glaze with yellow lake.

CHAPTER VI.

DISTEMPER OR TEMPERA PAINTING.

THE word distemper has a distinct interpretation in its connection with the brightening and embellishing of our buildings. Its Italian derivation, *tempera*, gives at once a key to its meaning, when compared with the word tempering: to temper, to work up, or to mix. Notwithstanding that this mixing, or tempering, is a process common to all painting, oil and otherwise, *tempera* is the recognised name for *water painting:* that is to say, the compounding and spreading of *opaque* solids and pigments with water for the solvent, and some suitable *vehicle* introduced to bind the particles together.

It is a process seldom used in this country, except for ceilings; but the Italian painters use it freely, and execute really excellent decorations with it. At the South Kensington Museum, altar-pieces, covered with decorative pictures with hundreds of figures in them, are painted in distemper. It is common for painters to work their distemper as if it were oil colour, but its nature is entirely different. Distemper might with advantage be used in bedrooms, on account of its cleanliness, the facility with which it can be removed, and its healthsome qualities; and cleanliness of walls is a most important matter in every house, especially during hot weather, when so much dirt and dust cling to them, endangering life and health at every respiration by reason of the germs of disease contained on unclean walls. With colouring matter cheaper than paper, people might easily purify and brighten their own walls, as indeed they commonly do north of the Tweed.

In the present day, the qualities and cheapness of distemper make it as valuable to the decorator as are oil and flatting paint. For preservative purposes, and as a covering for surfaces exposed to our humid atmosphere and weather, distemper is, however, practically useless ; and although under fair conditions it will stand some wear and tear on walls, it is principally in situations out of reach and beyond abrasion where it is used with more advantage than oil paint. The most satisfactory purpose to which to apply either oil paint or distemper will readily be apparent if we consider their totally distinct qualities and nature. In the former mixture, whilst the linseed oil is the solvent, it is also the binding factor, driers being added merely to hasten and accentuate the hardening. In distemper colour, the solvent—water—has no such permanent action as has the oil in the former, but it is entirely dispersed and carried away by evaporation.

It therefore follows that distemper, besides being prepared from dry pigment with water to enable us to manipulate it, requires a third and highly important factor which shall of itself bind the particles together, and hold them in position when evaporation is complete.

The leading characteristic of distemper is absence of gloss, and it is suited solely for interior and unexposed situations ; yet many attempts have been made to combine its cheapness with the permanent qualities of oil paint.

Before distemper work was so common as size and size powders and improved pigments have of late years made it, the walls of apartments were sometimes painted in tempera, and finished, at some expense, by polishing or satining with French chalk and flat brushes. Nowadays, however, this is very seldom done directly on wall surfaces, although a similar process is still used on some paper-hangings. Excess of vehicle in distemper, whether gum, glue, or size, causes it to crack and peel off ; so that even though an egg-shell gloss could be obtained, were sufficient used, it would only be at the sacrifice of permanence. The ancient *tempera* work of the days of the Pharaohs was, presumably, painted on in water, and afterwards covered with wax

By the addition of hot oil or Russian tallow, a mixture, with lime or whiting for its body, can be made to stand rain and weather on outsides; but such a mixture would be unfit for fine interior work. Any absorbent *tempera* paint is certainly preferable to oil paint for the insides of public buildings. Tempera absorbs the atmospheric moisture, and then gives it up again; whilst with oil paint, the moisture condenses on the surface and trickles down the walls.

Mixtures of distemper—that is, size and whiting—with turps, hot linseed oil, Russian tallow, etc., are occasionally made to spread on outside work, and are successful so far as they contain the oil or grease which repels the water. For inside work, a washable tempera is impossible from ordinary ingredients, and without chemical processes. There are, however, a few so-called washable distempers in the market which, as *washable* paints, are fairly successful; but since they are prepared from a basis other than whiting, they lack considerably the opacity that can be obtained with one coat of good plain distemper.

In oil and distemper painting there is in each one substance which ranks for binding purposes above all others. This position is held for oil paint by the ordinary *white lead*, and other similar carbonates; but these latter are seldom required for ordinary house-painting. For *tempera* painting, we are provided with an unlimited store of limestone and chalk, from which the ordinary lime, *oxide of calcium*, of building processes, and a further preparation known as *carbonate of lime*, are obtained.

In distemper painting—more frequently called colouring—the base generally used for all the tints is finest whiting.

Whiting—or whitening as it is sometimes termed—is the most ordinary and also the most useful form of carbonate of lime. Paris white and gilders' whiting are the best qualities of the same article, and differ from the cheap kind in fineness of substance and purity of white. Paris white is in great demand in the United States of

America, where, under the term of kalsomining, the practice of whitewashing is carried to perfection. Repeated grinding and washing are resorted to in order to convert the chalk into the condition of whiting, the processes being worked to extremes when the finer qualities are required.

It may be mentioned that Paris white is usually sold in a loose or powdered form, whilst gilders' whiting is commonly dried in the form of knobs, each weighing 3 or 4 lbs., and being, therefore, about twice the size of the knobs sold at oil-shops.

Whiting that has been properly washed and prepared will easily break in the hands by pressure of the fingers; and there should also be a total absence of grit and sand. Not to crumble up and dissolve easily is evidence that insufficient washing has left objectionable traces of a binding nature, common to lime. Upon the purity of the whiting much of the permanency and beauty of the *tints* of distemper will depend. Whiting which contains grit is entirely useless for the preparation of surfaces for *water-gilding;* whilst if present to any extent in distemper, grit will settle to the bottom of the vessel, and will often carry with it the bulk of any powdered pigment used for tinting or staining purposes.

Until recent years, the ordinary glue of commerce was the only serviceable "binder," or water-vehicle, convenient to house-painters for making distemper. To the present day, glue is still largely used in the provinces and places remote from the larger trade centres. The usual mode of preparation is to soak it in cold water over night, and then, by breaking it up with the hand or the application of heat, to convert it into a liquid or jelly form, when it is ready for adding to the whiting. The advantage of thus using and preparing glue lies in being able to stock it without deterioration. In all large towns, glue for distemper purposes is now entirely superseded by size—a jelly substance, of similar source and nature.

Size, or *Clear-cole,* is merely liquid glue, being

generally prepared by boiling down the sinewy and horny parts of animals, the strongest being obtained from the oldest animals. These substances are purified with lime and the gelatinous matter extracted by gradual boiling, and the clarified condition of this extract is the *size*. When required to be converted into glue, this liquid, after the greater portion of the water has been evaporated, cools into a very strong jelly. It is then divided into blocks, which are ultimately converted into cakes of hard glue by a double process of drying by natural and artificial methods. What is called *double size* is merely a stronger concoction, obtained by boiling it down to about half the quantity. When used by itself as a *priming*, or first coat, to fill up or cover over the surface of a porous material like plaster, it is called *clair-cole*, or *clear-cole*. Size is also mixed with whiting and colouring matters, to make them adhere to surfaces without rubbing off as readily as whitewash does.

Clear, or *Gilders'*, *Size* is made by simmering parchment cuttings in a vessel—preferably with an enamelled inside—until the gelatinous virtue is all extracted. It is then poured off in its liquid state and strained through fine muslin, and when cool, is almost colourless. Clear size is one of the most important used in all water-gilding processes; knowledge of and practice in it are very essential to such work. Gilders who are masters of every branch of the craft, and who follow it entirely as their trade, always prepare their own clear size. It is also used for finishing decorative oil gilding, and the decorator should also know how to prepare it.

Painters' size is usually sold by the pound weight, or in firkins containing about 28 lbs. The finest and whitest variety is known as Patent Size, which for purity and strength is equal to any produced. *Double size* and *extra double* are the two qualities most used for distemper, the latter being the stronger; neither of these are to be compared with Young's for purity and translucency, their darker colour being similar to that of size prepared from ordinary glue of good quality.

These jelly sizes are put into a vessel and dissolved by heat when required for use, a little water being first introduced to prevent the size from burning. Size should never be made very hot, but dissolved sufficiently only to allow of its being thoroughly incorporated with the whiting or other pigment. The disadvantage to the jelly form is its liability to putrefy and decompose during hot weather. For this reason glue is often substituted in the provinces and districts where the comparatively small demand for it does not warrant the trader or house-painter keeping it, and where there is no factory-made size at hand.

At the present time every glue and size factory makes a glue powder, size powder, or concentrated size, which is usually retailed in penny, quarter-, half-, and one-pound packets. By dissolving this powder in boiling water, according to the directions sold with it, a good binder for distemper work is provided without any of the risks or trouble attending the use of glue or the storing of size.

The best method of mixing distemper is to first put some cold water into the vessel in which the distemper is to be made, and then add the whiting into it, breaking up the lumps, so that, without any unnecessary delay, the whiting may be thoroughly dissolved. Care should be taken not to use too much water, sufficient only to cover the whiting being required. When properly slacked and settled down, the surplus water must be gently poured off. A careful worker will then thoroughly stir the whiting to ensure it being all properly dissolved: this is best done by the bare hand and arm.

Then gently pour in the warm size, and continue to stir and mix until the size and whiting become thoroughly worked together. This mixture should now be set aside in a cool place, when it will gradually assume a white jelly form. The amount of melted size used would be about half the bulk of the soaked whiting; but should there be an excess of water in the latter, it often so dilutes the size that there is not sufficient strength contained in the whole mixture to gelatinise or set it. To prevent a yellow shade in the whiting, grind a little indigo or ivory black in some water, and mix before adding the size, which has been previously warmed, well stirring the whole until properly mixed. Strain while warm, to remove impurities, and thoroughly mix the colour. Distemper should at all times be worked cold. Care should be taken not to have much pigment in it, otherwise the distemper will crack and fall off in scales; as it is not only the strength of the size that causes the work to crack, but also the body of colour.

Some readers may feel that this simple pail of whitewash requires more care in its preparation than was anticipated, but good work cannot be done with materials improperly prepared.

Very often in the very common kinds of whitewashing, on country cottage ceilings, etc., the housewife brushes over the surface whiting and water only, just as lime is used for white liming. Solid appearance is not produced with such material; and although for ceiling work less- proportion of size than that given above may be used, jelly distemper works easier, presents a more solid appearance, and is manipulated with less splashing and mess than is usual with the watery wash often used even by others than country house-wives.

Another method of mixing whiting for whitewash is in the proportion of 6 lbs. of whiting to 1 qt. of double size, the whiting to be just covered with cold water for six hours, then mixed with the hot size, and left in a cool place until it becomes like jelly, in which condition it is ready to be diluted with cold water, and used. It will take 1 lb. of this jelly to cover every six superficial yards.

Excess of size or glue in water colour will often give an "egg-shell" gloss, but the amount of size there must then be in the distemper will probably cause it to crack and peel off. Unless used upon walls, distemper is best with only sufficient size to bind it, and not to show any gloss whatever. The dead surface of distemper is one of its chief attractions. In former times, walls were sometimes distempered, and then polished with French chalk; but this is very seldom done now. The satin surface of some wall papers is obtained by such a process. Smoothness will depend upon the preparation of the distemper, the condition of the surface to be covered, and the skill in spreading it.

Those who have studied the chapter on mixing oil paints will have in their mind how far the condition of the surface to be covered affects proportions of material used in that process. The same principle underlies both oil and distemper work; and the success of the latter will greatly depend upon the preparation of the plaster surface. No break must be made in a piece of continuous work or flank of wall, but every surface complete in itself, like a ceiling-flat or side of a room, must be commenced and expeditiously completed without join or miss. A uniformity of absorption must therefore be ensured by previously coating the plaster with a mixture which, like the first thin coats of paint in oil painting, shall stop the unequal suction common to all bare plaster-work.

For this first coat, the most convenient preparation is strong jelly size diluted with about one-third of water, and just sufficient whiting to colour, without practically thickening, the size. This is termed clear-coat, or clear-cole, and it should be prepared in precisely the same manner as the finishing distemper; and the addition of a little alum is desirable. The hardening action of alum on substances of a gelatinous nature is well known; but the introduction of the alum is not obligatory. Strong size and whiting alone will suffice; and this should be applied warm, as soon as mixed, for when cold it would be too stiff to spread with the brush. No precautions concerning joins and streaks are required when using clear-cole, since there is not sufficient body in it to form an appreciable crust upon the wall. The size soaks into the face of the wall, and when dry, is ready for the finishing coat.

Occasionally, pure beeswax can be added to distemper with advantage for decorating ceilings in tempera. For painting or stencilling ornament upon, it forms a harder surface, without risk of peeling off. It can scarcely be termed washable, but may be made to stand a considerable amount of wear and cleaning. The mode of preparation is to dissolve pure yellow beeswax in oil of turpentine by heat, and to have the whiting ready for mixing with strong and very hot size, and well mixed together before stirring in the melted wax. This preparation of wax is not commended to novices, as the professional hand is needed to work it successfully.

About 4 ozs. of genuine yellow beeswax, having been scraped into shreds and dissolved in oil of turpentine, should be added to a half-bucketful of distemper, in order to make a *tempera* paint for good decorative work; or for a fair-sized pailful the proportions would be $\frac{1}{2}$ lb. pure beeswax in $1\frac{1}{2}$ pints of turps, the two well mixed, and then added as directed.

In America, wall colouring in distemper is called kalsomining, and it is best done when the walls are neither very cold nor very hot. But it may be done during the winter, so long as the walls do not freeze. There are a good many preparations made for this purpose, and sold under various names. White kalsomine may be prepared in the following manner :—10 lbs. best whiting, $1\frac{1}{2}$ lbs. white glue, $\frac{1}{2}$ lb. alum, and a little ultramarine blue. Put the glue to soak for twelve hours in cold water, then set it on the fire, and stir until dissolved. Put about half a-gallon of cold water over the whiting, and when dissolved, add the glue, the blue, and the alum, which must have been dissolved in hot water. Stir this mixture well, and strain through a sieve. This may be used while hot for first coating, but the other coats must be cold. If it works too stiff, a little soap will help. All colours and shades are made by adding the dry colours.

Before kalsomining, cracks and nail holes should be filled with plaster of Paris. Mix this with flour paste, and it will not dry so quickly. Use a good brush, and work as quickly as possible, to avoid laps, to make a good job of kalsomining. A neat stencil border run around the top of the wall makes a nice finish.

Another recipe is :—15 lbs. best whiting or French kalsomine, dissolved in cold water, and 1 lb. of fine white glue dissolved in water. Apply cold. For very fine white work, zinc white is preferred to whiting, but as the expense is so much greater it is seldom used. Half-an-ounce of ultramarine blue added to the above gives a clearer white. Pigments may be added to colour to suit, but all colouring must be put in before adding the glue.

Lines of colour may be run with lining-fitch and straight-edge upon paper, distemper, or such-like absorbent surface either as size colour or turps colour. For size colour, mix best Venetian red powder with water to a stiff paste, then thin for use with strong jelly size. This must be kept warm in using, as you may surmise. For turps colour, use Japan gold size to make the dry pigment into batter consistency, then thin for use with turps. Both of these should work well and stand sizing.

In all preparations of paint the purity of tints of colours is very much dependent upon that of the body pigment used. As good whiting is more white and brilliant than white lead, it follows that purer and more delicate tints may be obtained in distemper work than is possible with substances more affected by the atmosphere, as are the carbonates of lead and oils which develop yellowness.

If gilders' or Paris whiting be used with *clear* or Young's patent size, the purity of distemper tints is very much in advance of those of white lead.paint, so that it is impossible to match them in oil colour. In choosing the paint to suit the colour of the paper of a room, this fact must be borne in mind, and allowance made for it. Exact matching in oil and water is not necessary. Colours should always be judged by the general or dominant effect, and not by any small portion

The pigment used for tinting, or colouring, distemper, whether ground in water or in powder form, should be mixed with the whiting before the size is added. It cannot otherwise be properly worked into the whiting, and after the size is added the distemper should be strained through a thin gauze or hair sieve. Straining it after getting set will give it in a condition very agreeable for spreading.

The nature of distemper is such that its tints are very much lighter when dry than when first spread. This is due to the action of light upon the water used for mixing. The evaporation of this causes the pigment to convey a less bright sensation than it did before becoming dry.

In mixing distemper tints, accustom the mind to judging the effect of a colour when dry. Avoid all plain tints of white with pure red, blue, yellow, green, etc. Make up the various tones of colour in the pots; then put a little red into green, green into red, etc., until they are sufficiently soft and neutralised to give a restful and harmonious combined effect.

All the pigments used for distemper paint should either be ground very fine or should be washed so as to ensure the most minute division of their particles. Two coats, and sometimes more, of any tint will be required to cover plaster well, and to dry out with absolute uniformity.

The pigments should be mixed separately, and should be carefully added to the white body. Powder pigment should never be added dry to the body white. Sufficient material of any particular tint as may be required for one room or job should be compounded at once, to avoid the trouble of matching. If only a small quantity of any additional pigment is required, it should be well ground on a slab, and taken on the point of the palette-knife or at the end of a stick, and thus mixed with the general mass.

Great care must be taken in mixing pigments, for some, such as Prussian blue, etc., are so strong that a very little will produce the desired effect; and if they are used in excess, it becomes necessary to add more and more white, a greater quantity of the material required is compounded and waste results.

The pigments most suitable for staining whiting will be gathered from the chapter on pigments, but a few of the most useful and ordinary are appended :—For warm red tints, Venetian and Indian reds and burnt sienna ; for buffs, cinnamons, etc., the natural ochres, umbers, and siennas with the above reds. Lime blue and so-called ultramarine make blue and grey, with red added for French grey, and blue-black or Paris black where the neutral is required. Greens are seldom required bright, and mixtures of raw sienna or ochre with lime blue, indigo, or ultramarine are most reliable. All dark-colour distemper paints, such as purple-brown, for instance, seldom require whiting, only the pigment prepared in a similar manner. All mixtures should be tested and dried on paper to judge the colour ; and when this is correct, add the hot size.

In order to produce an absolutely level tint in distemper, great care should be exercised in carrying on the work. Whilst the colour is being laid on, the windows and doors should be closed and all draughts prevented, so that the wash may not dry too quickly, in which case the brush drags, and all piecings or brush marks will show when quite dry; but the moment the work is finished all windows and doors are to be opened, in order to afford free ingress to the fresh air, for as soon as the whole of the colour is laid on, the sooner it dries the better.

In distempering walls where a good job is required, the stopping and clear-coling must be carefully performed and thoroughly dry before the finishing coat, in a nicely jellied condition, is spread. In covering a wall of ordinary height, two workers are necessary, one standing on the scaffold and taking from the top, half-way down, the other working beneath him. It is a good plan for the bottom man to start spreading and keep slightly ahead of his fellow, who then, in his laying off strokes, will cover all traces of the join.

CHAPTER VII.

WHITEWASHING AND DECORATING A CEILING.

THE greater number of plaster ceilings are finished with distemper paint, which, besides the advantages of cheapness and of covering in one coat, where with oil paint four would be required, shows superiority in other respects.

In places where people congregate, the moisture in the atmosphere—unless the ventilation of the apartment is exceptionally good—will condense upon a painted surface and run down the walls. When distemper is used in such situations, no unpleasant effect is seen, since the distempered surface will absorb the moisture for the time being, and ultimately give it forth again without any detriment to its colour.

This property of distemper also indicates the necessity of removing, with brushes and water, all old colouring and whitewash from ceiling and walls, instead of which, the dirty unhealthy coating is in some cases coated over with size. The size binds the dirt, and the opacity of distemper paint does not show the dirt through; nevertheless, it is a practice to be condemned by all who desire sanitary homes. Doubtless this labour-saving plan would be used even to a more general extent but for the fact that continuous coats of distemper and size soon discover the bad worker by the surface cracking and peeling off, owing to excess of size.

When about to whitewash a ceiling, the first thing is to have the room as clear as possible, and to protect the wall-paper tack a width of old newspapers round the walls half an inch from the ceiling. The best way to tack the paper up is to cut some ordinary corks into slices about a quarter of an inch thick, and to drive the tacks through these into the plaster.

Next with hot water thoroughly wash off from the ceiling the old distemper or whiting, being careful to wash only the ceiling, and not to let the dirty water run down the wall-paper nor splash about.

It is important to have a scaffold-board at such a height from the floor that the ceiling can be comfortably reached. Have at each end of the board a pair of steps, though two chairs will answer the purpose; or even a table alone will serve. Now, with a pail of clean hot water, a distemper brush, a large piece of sponge, and a piece of coarse canvas on a board or table beside you, start at one corner of the room to lay or soak in a patch with water, gently stirring the old distemper with the brush. Get the old distemper thoroughly soaked, then wash it off with the canvas, finishing with the sponge, frequently rinsed in water. This is to get rid of every trace of the old distemper or whitewash. This is a most important process, which cannot be too strongly insisted upon. Neglect in this part of the work will result in a dirty or uneven appearance in the finished ceiling. Old lime is difficult to remove, but all of it must be got off. If only the loose portions are removed, even the most skilful application of distemper cannot hide the patches. They will be either of a different colour or else will show the shade from a different level of surface. Do not wet the surface more than necessary, and frequently change the water as it gets dirty. Sometimes the distemper is especially difficult to get off on account of the original coat having been bound down, as it is called, instead of having been washed off before it was last re-whitened, which is very often done for the sake of cheapness. Twopennyworth of liquid ammonia in a separate pail half full of water will greatly assist when soaking bound distemper. Avoid touching the wall-paper with the brush, but finish the last inch or so of margin with the sponge or canvas.

When the surface of the ceiling has dried, any rough

patches there may be should be scraped or rubbed smooth.

If there are any cracks in the ceiling, run the point of a small trowel along them, to clear out any loose bits, dust, etc., with a sash-tool wet the parts of the ceiling where the cracks are, and then, using a stopping-knife, fill them in with plaster of Paris mixed with water in which a little alum has been dissolved. A little whiting mixed with the plaster will keep it from setting too quickly.

Or mix fine plaster of Paris with glue size, and fill up holes and cracks, and when dry level with a knife or coarse glass-paper. Whiting mixed with glue water would also be suitable. Use a square piece of wood to mix the cement upon, and nail a handle to the other side.

If the cracks are at all bad, they should be cut out, the face of the plaster on each side cut away for half an inch, and the gap then finished to a level surface with plaster laid on with a small trowel. A broad thin strip of wood with a bevelled edge is very useful when stopping plaster walls, for in trying to stop a crack or hole with a sharp steel stopping knife, the surrounding face of the plaster may be badly scratched, which is only seen when the job is finished.

Repairing should be done to new ceilings before the clear-cole is applied, and to old ceilings at the time they are washed off—that is, when the old coating of dirty distemper is removed with water and brushes.

If necessary, when dry, the ceiling can be rubbed quite smooth with glass-paper, and is then ready for re-distempering, after which, if carefully done, the repaired cracks will be invisible.

If there are stains in the ceiling that cannot be removed by washing, the stain should be painted white, in flat colour or paint mixed with turpentine. If this has to be done, it will be well to paint also the filling with which the cracks have been stopped.

Finally, the ceiling should be rubbed down with a cloth previous to applying the colour.

To prepare whitewash, break into large pieces about four balls of whiting, and put them into a pail, and just cover the material with water; let it stand all night. In the morning, pour off all water that will run away, and thoroughly mix the wet whiting by hand until it becomes a thick even paste. Add about half an egg-cupful of dry ultramarine blue, stirring it well in with the whiting. Next put 2 lbs. of Young's patent size in a saucepan over the fire, with only just sufficient water to keep it from burning, and stirring it all the time, taking great care that it neither boils nor burns. When it is thoroughly dissolved, pour it on the whiting, and mix the whole well together. The proportion of size is about one tea-cupful to two gallons of the mixture. If a perfectly white wash is required, potato starch may be used. Now set it aside in a cool place until it turns to a jelly. When it is quite cold, with a distemper brush rub it through a coarse piece of canvas stretched over the top of a clean pail, and it will then be ready for use.

Before commencing the actual whitewashing, lightly rub over the whole of the ceiling with a piece of fine glass-paper, to take off any little knots or brush-hairs left by the clear-coling. Then dust the ceiling before proceeding to whiten it.

In laying on the wash, a large flat brush is employed, and if this is not over-charged, a ceiling or wall may with a certain amount of care be white- or colour-washed with little or no splashing. The way to lay the distemper on is not to take up too much in the brush, and not to flick the brush at the end of each stroke, or you will splash everything. Work the brush in any direction, but be sure that every part of the ceiling is covered with distemper, taking care to keep the edges of the patches going—that is, do not let any edge get dry before you come to it again. To do this, it is essential to have a scaffold that is easily movable from one end of the room to the other. The whitening must be done very expeditiously; and any ceiling over 14 ft. square should not be attempted single-handed without some previous practice.

Ceilings should always be distempered by working away *from* the light. Two men are required to do a good-sized ceiling-flat; they should start at the window end, and, keeping their work in one general line, spread the distemper from the end as far towards the centre as they can both conveniently reach. The scaffold is then brought forward and another shift covered, and so on until the whole ceiling is finished. The solvent used for distemper work being water, it will be seen that extreme heat or a draught of air, such as will evaporate the water, is to be avoided during the process; but so soon as a ceiling is completed, the object is to *dry* it off as *quickly* as possible; and hence it is well to open door and window, to create the draught we previously had to avoid.

Properly executed distempering should have a level, but not perfectly smooth, surface, which should show no joins or coarse brush-markings, and should have a perfectly dead appearance, be solid and uniform throughout, and should *not* rub off by ordinary wear or leaning against.

Distemper of any kind should never be spread over old or dirty stuff; these should be first washed off. An expert will not flap his brush in working well-made distemper; he will use the tip of his brush only, and make very little noise. Whitewash or any distemper can be laid on in any direction *from* the outer or working edge. Splashes result from the use of watery wash and want of experience in working; and they are avoided by the use of *jellied* stuff.

A distemper brush should be worn off a trifle before being used to whiten a ceiling. The work of washing off a ceiling will be sufficient to wear down a new brush to a fit condition. After the brush is done with, wash it out thoroughly and lay it by; before attempting to use it, soak it in water, or the hairs may fall out, through it being too dry. This last caution applies to nearly all brushes used in house decorating.

If there is a delicate ornamental cornice in the room that cannot be got at with the ordinary distemper brush, described on p. 65, a smaller brush, called a distemper tool, is used both for the washing off and whitening. In the whitening, push this brush up into the ornamented parts as you would use a stencil brush; but it does not much matter how the distemper is laid so long as it is put on evenly, and all the surface covered.

There appears to be an idea that a new ceiling requires some special treatment before it is whitened; but this is not so. Providing that the ceiling has been left by the plasterer in a proper condition, it is a more simple job than whitening an old one, on account of there being no washing-off or making-good to do. The most ordinary cause of failure is that the ceilings are not thoroughly dry before the whitewash is put on. If there is the least sign of sweating or moisture on the ceiling, it may be taken to indicate that the ceiling is not dry; and if this is so, no amount of care in making or putting on the whitewash will make the ceiling white. Another cause of failure may be due to the fact that some people do not consider it necessary to clear-cole a new ceiling. This is also a mistake, for the clear-cole stops absorption, and if there is a little whiting in it, it helps to cover, and, moreover, makes the distempering a much easier job, as it prevents it dragging, and, to use a painter's term, the distemper spreads like butter. The addition of a little alum is also an improvement to the clear-cole. But the advantages of using the jellied preparation cannot be too strongly impressed upon users of distemper.

To Distemper a Ceiling in Pink.—Obtain a pail of well-washed whiting, 1½ lbs. best concentrated size, and two-pennyworth of best Venetian red. Put the Venetian red into a tin with enough water to cover it, and then put it on one side to soak. Now get two clean pails and a stirring-stick. Break open the size packets and tip the contents into one of the pails. Add about three pints of water to it, and stir up well with a stick; stand that on one side. Place a kettle of water on the fire, as some boiling water will shortly be required.

Half fill another pail with water, and holding each lump of whiting over the pail, break the whiting into it by gently tapping with a small hammer. There are now two pails: one containing size, and the other whiting. Pour the boiling water in upon the size, stirring all the time, and then stand the mixture on one side to cool. With your hand now thoroughly break up the whiting in the other pail. It ought to be made of the consistency of thin glazing putty. Put a little of it on a piece of paper, to compare the coloured wash with when tinting. The Venetian red, which ought to be well soaked, can now be added to the whiting in small quantities, and testing the result every time by comparing with the whiting placed on the paper. If doubtful as to whether the correct tint is obtained, dry a little of the wash on a piece of paper in front of the fire, keeping the distempered side away from and the clean side towards the fire. Place the paper on your ceiling, and fix it there with a pin. Go out and have a look at the grass, or anything green, for a minute or two. Come back and quickly look at the sample colour, and decide whether it suits. When the tint has been obtained, add the size, which ought to be cool, but not cold, by this time, and stir well with your hand. It will become very stiff for a minute or two, so that you will hardly be able to stir it. Add more size to it until in appearance it becomes like good oil paint, then strain it carefully into another clean pail. Return about a quart of it into the first pail, and add the rest of the size to this, which ought to make a very thin and strong mixture. Now add to this also about a tablespoonful of ground alum; stir well, and this is now "clear-cole."

To the pail of distemper gently pour one cupful of cold water on top, so as to prevent a skin from coming on as it chills. Cover it over, and put it away in the cool till chilled—which will be on the next day, most likely. If the ceiling be dry, go over it with the clear-cole, so that it will be dry for the distemper next morning. Get someone to help you; do not attempt it by yourself. Begin nearest to the light, and work from it, covering centre ornament first, bed of ceiling next, and cornice last. Coat the bed in strips 2 ft. in width, and when a shift is made, go along the edge of the strip of distemper last put on, and soften well into it. If the day be fine, throw open your windows when finished.

Any colour can be obtained by first preparing a wash as for ordinary whitewashing, and then mixing in colouring matter until the desired tint is obtained. For pink, use rose pink; for salmon, Venetian red; for lilac, a

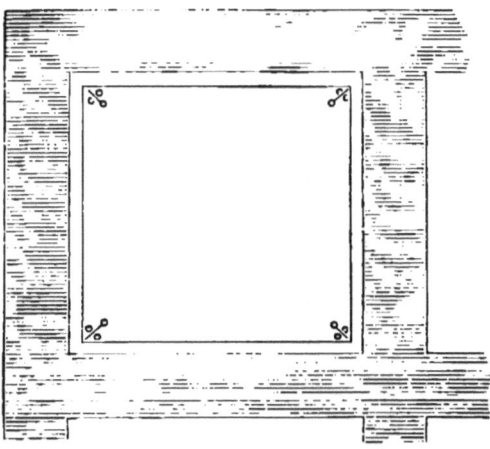

Fig. 56.—Ceiling divided into four simple Panels.

little indigo and rose pink; for grey, lamp-black; for French grey, Prussian blue and lake; for blue, Prussian blue, indigo, or cobalt; for green, emerald green; for buff, yellow ochre; for drab, burnt or raw umber. A beginner should mix a small quantity at first, and apply a patch, and when it is dry an estimate can be made of the effect. These colours usually dry lighter.

To thoroughly clean a Room.—Every particle of old paper should be stripped off, and everything washed off the walls with hot soda-water until the plaster is left quite clean. If there are vermin confined to certain spots, saturate the parts well with carbolic acid; or petroleum is useful. If general, give the walls—after all holes and crevices are stopped with plaster of Paris—a coat of strong patent or glue size with some carbolic acid or turpentine in it (about 1 gill to 1 gallon of size).

In the majority of houses the ceiling presents a plain flat expanse of white, without anything to relieve its monotony; sometimes a cornice is run round the room, which improves it a little, but in very few cases is anything done to improve the remaining portion of the

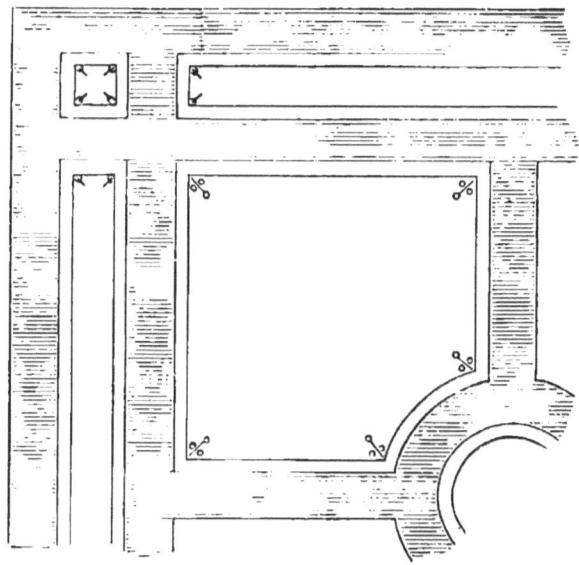

Fig. 57.—Ceiling with Circular Centre.

ceiling. The following pages show how, by a very little extra expenditure, the appearance of the ceiling may be greatly improved.

After the ceiling is whitewashed and dry, with a chalk line make a mark 6 in. from the cornice or walls, and get some narrow wall-paper bordering of suitable colour, and paste it on to the chalk lines, putting corner pieces at the angles; the bordering should be 1 in. or 1½ in. wide, and should be put on quite straight. If desired, the space between the bordering and cornice may be tinted.

Or instead of using the bordering, colour a margin 6 in. wide all round the ceiling, and at a distance of 1 in. or 1½ in. from this paint a line of chocolate ⅜ in. or ½ in. wide all round, and stencil an ornamental pattern at each angle. The edge of the coloured margin should be kept perfectly straight, and the chocolate lines should be painted to a rule or straight-edge held against the ceiling.

If there be a cornice, it should have been washed, the

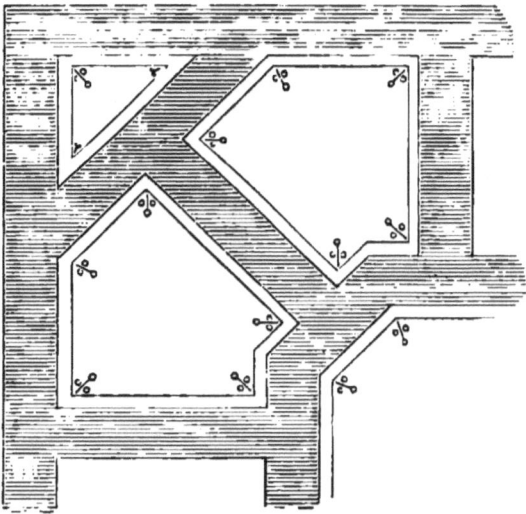

Fig. 58.—Ceiling with Octagonal Centre.

cracks filled up, and whitewashed in the same manner as the ceiling. The cove, or large hollow, may be tinted the same colour as the margin on the ceiling, but the other members of the cornice will look better white, as when tinted it gives the cornice a heavy appearance.

If the ceiling is large, it may be divided into four panels, as shown in Fig. 56, the shaded part representing the colour. The width of the margins may also be increased in a large ceiling.

Fig. 57 shows another method of dividing a ceiling into panels, a circular margin being formed in the centre, round the chandelier.

Before laying the colour on, it should be tried on some surface and allowed to dry; as if made too dark the ceiling will have a heavy appearance. Pink or salmon colour will be found very suitable for the margins, although others may be used; the stringing lines and

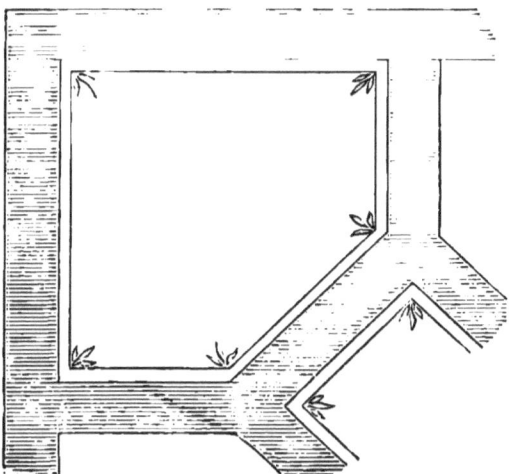

Fig. 59.—Ceiling with Square Central Panel.

stencilling will look best in chocolate, or some similar dark colour.

Figs. 58 and 59 show two other methods of dividing the ceiling which have a very good appearance. The centre portion of the panels may also be tinted, if desired, to a very light shade of the colour used in the margins; but when the room is low it is advisable to have the colours light, while for a lofty room, well lighted, a darker shade is sometimes an improvement. Each drawing in Figs. 56, 57, 58, and 59 represents one-fourth of the ceiling.

CHAPTER VIII.

PAINTING A ROOM.

The first step in distempering is to obtain a clear surface upon which to work; and in oil painting also it is necessary first of all to remove, as far as possible, all old coats of paint, so that the new shall have as good a foundation as can be obtained. Old paint is often removed with a charcoal-burner, but there are other methods more likely to be within reach. A mixture of soft soap and water, with plenty of soda added, is a fairly good paint remover.

The following recipes will be found useful and more effective :—Take 1 lb. American pearlash and 3 lbs. quick stone lime; slack the lime in water, then add the pearlash, and make the whole about the consistence of paint. Cover the surface of old paint with the mixture, applying it with a sash-tool, and let it remain several hours. If necessary, give a second coat. Or coat the paint with naphtha, repeating if necessary; usually one coat is sufficient to soften the old paint so that it can be scraped off. The lime and soda method is a good one, and if used to remove paint from wood that is afterwards to be stained is perhaps the best. To make the preparation, put three parts of quicklime and one part of common soda into a pail, and pour boiling water over it, to form a paste when slaked. Spread this paste with a palette or broad knife over the paint to be removed. After standing a few hours, the paint will become soft; scrape off, and wash well with cold water. When dry, give the surface a coat of weak acid, if it is intended to re-paint it. The object of this coat of acid (which should be applied with a brush, as in painting) is to kill the chemical action of any of the alkali solvent that may be still left in the grain of the wood, and which would be liable to perish the new paint, etc., put upon it.

This last method is better than firing for removing paint from mouldings and other irregular surfaces, since with the charcoal-burner the prominent parts would get burned before the heat could perish the paint in the recessed parts.

If, however, it is desired to employ the burning process, a useful and reliable spirit-lamp should be obtained. The Paquelin (patent) is a simple contrivance, of which any parts may be renewed. Its chief advantages are: burning in any position, its great heat, simplicity of use, and lightness. The cost of working it is about a halfpenny per hour. The usual difference in the appearance of burnt-off work is that some of the priming remains in the grain of the wood, and therefore the surface would not be so absorbent as the lime-treated portion, and it would be hardly possible to get a uniform colour.

Varnish may be removed from wood-work by applying as a solvent a mixture of equal parts of turpentine and alcohol.

In cases where it is only necessary to clean—not to remove—paint, a strong solution of soda will generally do all that is required. Some use a pickle compound of soda and slaked lime, but the soda solution will, however, be found quite strong enough for general paint-cleaning purposes, especially if applied hot; but do not use it too strong, or it will fetch paint (and varnish also) off wholesale. Some painters moisten grease spots with turps, and then pumice and wash off with clean water only.

All surfaces which are to be painted should be thoroughly dry, clean, smooth, and free from dust. When new wood is to be painted, the first operation is called knotting, the object of which is to prevent stains appearing upon the finished work by the turpentine exuding from the knots in the wood. There are various methods of effecting this. The preparation generally used is composed of shellac dissolved in naphtha, and is known as patent knotting. This operation may also be performed by covering the defective part with a composition formed of red lead and a small proportion of white lead and whiting made into a thin paste with size. Knots are sometimes covered with gold-leaf—a certain prevention, almost always adopted in best work. Another mode is to cut out the knot to the depth of about ¼ in., and to fill up the hole thus made with a hard stopping, composed of white lead with one-third of japan, and sufficient turpentine to make a stiff putty, or to cut out the knot altogether and fill with clear grained wood. This composition will become hard in about a quarter of an hour; but it should be left for twenty-four hours, then it should be rubbed down. It may then be painted over with confidence. The opening made by cutting away the knot must be painted before applying the composition; otherwise, it will not adhere, but will fall out immediately it becomes dry.

Knots may be painted with hot lime, and ironed with a hot iron when dry, and then painted smooth; or the lime may be left on for twenty-four hours, scraped off, and painted with red and white lead and linseed oil, and after this is thoroughly dry, smoothed with pumice-stone. Where time is more precious, patent knotting may be used. It dries in from five to ten minutes, forming a skin over the knots, thus allowing the painting to be proceeded with without loss of time. Where the knots are very bad and show through the third coat or second coat after priming, they should be covered with silver-leaf. This is done by laying on a coat of gold-size, and, when tacky, a silver-leaf is placed on, which is sure to prevent the knots appearing.

The next process is *priming*. This consists in laying the first coat of paint, the object being to diminish the absorbent quality of the material to be painted. This coat generally consists of red lead, or red lead and a small proportion of white lead, raw linseed oil, a little litharge; and a proper proportion of some drier is also added. Red lead has greater hardening properties than any other pigment used in painting, and, being applied to the work fresh from the carpenter's hands, the wood absorbs the priming readily, which gives it a harder surface as a basis for successive coats. Various tints are used by various persons, the red lead being put in haphazard, apparently under the impression that so long as it contains some, quantity is immaterial. To serve its purpose best, the priming coat should be of a deep salmon colour, and used much thinner than ordinary paint, the colouring matter being red lead only, and not Venetian red, as is sometimes employed. Priming must be done before *stopping* the work, the reason being that, if introduced before the first coat of colour is laid on, the putty used in the process of stopping will become quite loose when dry. The more white lead used in priming, the better it enters the pores of the wood. For inside work, it is composed of red and white lead ground, and mixed with linseed oil only. When dry, the work is rubbed down with glass-paper or pumice-stone, and all nail-holes are stopped with putty.

The following coats are termed second colour, third colour, etc., and contain about as much oil as turps. The last is termed the ground, and is nearly the colour of the intended finish, except for green, black, and some other colours, for which the ground is lead colour.

The almost useless practice of priming with clear-cole or glue size instead of oil is sometimes resorted to to save expense. Clear-cole should not be used in best work, as it does not enter or become absorbed in the pores of the surface operated upon, but simply forms a thin skin on the surface only; hence it is liable to crack and drop off. Clear-cole should not be used except in old work, the surface of which may be so dirty or so greasy as to prevent the proper drying of oil priming. When thoroughly dry, the priming should be rubbed down with glass-paper.

After the priming is dry, the next process is called stopping, and consists of filling up and making good nail holes, cracks, joints, etc., with putty or a mixture of putty and white lead. This operation is done with the stopping-knife.

Having made good all defects and seen that the work has been properly rubbed smooth, the colouring coats are applied. The brush should be held at right angles to the face of the work, so that only the ends of the hairs touch it, in order to force the paint into the pores of the material, and spread it evenly over the surface, without leaving streaky marks. In good work, each coat when dry should be well rubbed down with glass-paper or pumice-stone, and well dusted before applying the next coat.

The brushes and all the utensils should be freed from all dry paint by carefully scraping with a knife and washing with warm water; otherwise, the colours will soon become foul, and the work will be very inferior. The paint should be strained free from skins and all extraneous matter. In oil painting, the utmost cleanliness is requisite. With the ordinary paints, new wood or iron-work requires four coats, including the priming coat, but exclusive of any flatting coat; and old paint should have two coats for inside and three for outside work.

If it is intended that the work should have four coats of paint, it will be found desirable that there be in the second coat some approach to the colour required. If three coats are to be given, it would be found indispensable. The second coat should be diluted with about one-third turps, while the third coat should be mixed with oil and turps in equal proportions. For the fourth coat, one-third of oil to two-thirds of turps should be used. The second coat for new work is made up chiefly with oil, as it best stops the suction of the wood; but second coat for old work is made up chiefly with turpentine, because oil paint would not dry or adhere to it so well.

As a general direction, when applying the colour, it may be stated that the panel should be covered with a brush not over-charged with paint; and when laying paint there cannot be too little of it in the brush, or it will ooze out in one place as it is taken up in another. The paint should be spread on as evenly as possible ; and to effect this, as soon as the whole or a convenient quantity is covered, the brush should be passed over it in a direction contrary to that in which it is finally to be laid off. This is called crossing. After crossing, the surface should be laid off softly and carefully in the direction contrary to the crossings : that is with the grain of the wood, taking care that none of the cross brush marks remain visible.

The criterion of good workmanship is that the paint is laid evenly and the brush marks are not observable. In laying off, the brush should be laid upon that portion of the work already coated, so that the joining may not be perceived. Every coat should be perfectly dry, and all dust carefully removed before the succeeding one is laid over it. When the second coat is thoroughly dry and hard, it is advisable that the work should be rubbed down with glass-paper and carefully examined, to ascertain whether any further stopping or facing is required.

Flatting is resorted to more especially in good work, the object being the avoidance of the glossy surface appearance of oil paint. Work which is to have three coats and a *flat* must be grounded with a colour a few shades darker than that in which it is to be finished. The flatting must always be lighter than the ground, or, when finished, it would appear to consist of a series of shades and stripes. A uniform glossy surface is necessary to flat upon. A flatting coat consists of white lead, the requisite colouring matter, and turps, no oil being used. Sometimes a little copal varnish is added. Flatting must always be executed quickly, and the brush should be carried across the panel not more than once. The less the brush is used in flatting, the better it will appear when finished. Flatting will not allow of being washed, so it is not suitable for out-door work. In bastard flatting a small portion of size is added to the turps, to make a paint better capable of standing washing.

In dealing with old wood-work, such as boarded ceilings or wainscots, the difference in cost between painting it and re-distempering it will be very great. To properly paint it, it will first be necessary to wash off and scrape all the old whiting away from the wood, and then, when thoroughly dry, give it two coats of oily paint, which need not be white. This would stop the suction of the wood, and a decent job might then be made of the wood with two more good coats of white lead paint. Should this be too expensive a method, the following might suit the case. Thoroughly clean off the old accumulated whiting, and give two coats of white lead paint all over where the stains are; this will kill the stain, and a nice white surface can be obtained by distempering on the paint. The cheapest plan is to give the stained parts a thin coat of plaster of Paris and water, applied, like distemper, with an ordinary brush. This will very often kill a stain in an old plaster ceiling; but it is not always so effective as painting the stains, which is a certain remedy.

Sometimes the inexperienced painter will be annoyed by the ugly brown patches coming through the paint, even after three coats of white lead paint have been given. The trouble is generally very easily accounted for. It is the resin in the knots exuding from the wood discolouring the lead paint, owing to the inferior knotting used. The remedy is to give the places a thin coat, or two thin coats, of knotting composition: then make up the white paint—in proportions as before—with raw linseed instead of *boiled*. Then cover the knots twice with this paint, and give one coat all over to get once more a solid, uniform appearance. Four coats are none too many, so there will be no harm done.

When a plaster surface is to be covered with oil paint, a common practice is to prime with glue size, and then cover with four coats of colour, when the ordinary lead paints are used, and a flatting coat can be added if desired. A better plan is to apply a priming coat of boiled oil quite warm, and, when dry and hard, to add a thin coat of weak size, tinged with red lead, in order to stop absorption and to give the work a uniform tint. Finish off with two coats of oil paint, and a flatting colour if required ; or two coats of coloured varnish can be applied.

To guard against damp injuring the paint upon a plaster wall, it is safer to distemper the walls for the first two years, and then to wash it off and paint, taking care that the walls are perfectly dry. If the distemper is not greasy or dirty, it is better merely to brush it well down with a dry brush, and paint over it, without any washing.

Respecting cement wall-skirting, it is not generally advisable to paint until three days after finishing. If the roughing in mortar be thoroughly dry and hard, and a thin coating of Parian cement only skimmed over it, a day might be long enough before painting. Roughness is often caused, after a time, by chemical reaction of paint and wall.

The process of painting walls and ceilings in oil—called flatting—is one of the house-painter's most difficult operations. To ensure success, it must first be seen that the wall or the ceiling to be flatted is thoroughly dry.

It is then prepared by filling all holes and cracks with a stopping composed of plaster of Paris and glue size. The walls are then rubbed down with glass-paper, placed over a joiner's cork-block, to preserve evenness of surface. Priming should consist of one-third each of raw oil, boiled oil, and turpentine, mixed with white lead. Three coats of this should be given, allowing sufficient time to elapse between each coat to enable it to get dry and hard, and the fourth coat may be tinted to the colour required for flatting. The paint for flatting is prepared by mixing, in turpentine, white lead and the pigment required to form the tint desired, adding a little linseed oil ; the pigment is strained through muslin before use. The paint should be applied as rapidly as possible, as it is quick in setting, and should not be retouched. The stippling brush should be used evenly and gently, and one part finished before another is commenced. If a gloss is required, more oil must be used, and when done in this way it is called bastard flat, and is less liable to get soiled than true flatted work.

The length of time it is advisable to leave plaster work before painting or papering will vary according to different circumstances. Walls finished in white hard-faced cements, such as Keen's or Parian, can be painted a day or so afterwards. Walls finished with a large proportion of plaster in the finishing coat may be painted upon as soon as thoroughly dry, but it might be advisable to wait for some months before hanging papers containing pigments easily affected by lime. The ordinary skimming coat of small houses consists principally of lime putty.

New walls, as soon as dry, are often temporarily coated with distemper, which is tinted with some pigment not easily affected by lime : lime-blue, ochre, umber, and Venetian red are the most common and useful. But although these colours will withstand the lime action, this will, in less than six months, perish the size contained in the distemper. A whole year is the least time that can be safely advised before permanently papering or painting. Whether paint or paper is the better depends on circumstances.

Successive coats of paint must vary ; one flat coat of colour must not be laid upon another, but let the next be rather oily. A small quantity of varnish or of oil should be used to bind the flatting ; whichever is used as a binder, it is good to mix it overnight and to leave it twelve hours before using, so as to take the fire out of it. Some people close the doors and windows whilst at work, to retard the setting of the colour.

Varnishing should be done, as far as possible, in warm weather ; cold or damp chills the varnish. It should be laid on in short strokes and be evenly spread, care being taken not to re-touch any part once laid.

Extreme cleanliness need not be further urged. The object is to put the paint where it is required, and to avoid getting it on the hands or in the stocks of the brushes.

Have the colour bench as near as possible to the actual work, with a range of colours ready ground; or, if dry pigments are used, have them in bottles—not in pieces of paper, to be wasted all over the bench. The paint-pots should be cleaned every night.

Now, to apply the foregoing instructions in a thoroughly practical way, let us suppose that the reader has to finish a newly-built billiard-room. Furthermore, let us suppose that the apartment is principally lighted by a ceiling light; that the remainder of ceiling and the walls have been plastered with the usual finishing coat of lime-putty and plaster; that the enriched plaster cornice which frames the ceiling is of fine plaster, and the skirting and reveals of recessed windows are of Keen's or Parian cement; that the side windows are glazed with combined English sheet and ornamental coloured glass; and that the doors are of well-seasoned wood and properly hung.

Being assured that all the plaster work is thoroughly dry, we will proceed to finish it in oil paint, except the ceiling, which should be distempered. The plaster cornice, with its cast enrichment, is the most absorbent portion; next to this comes the wall space, which the trowelling to its surface has made rather less thirsty. The white and hard-faced cement skirting, made from Keen's or Parian, if well finished off, will absorb but very little oil, and must be treated accordingly.

Before getting a coat of lead upon them, it is necessary to stop the suction of cornice and walls; and to this end break up, with a small wooden spatula or flat stick, genuine white lead and the best patent driers, in proportions of about fourteen to one. With a little raw linseed oil, first get it to a thick batter, and when well broken up, reduce it to the thin working consistency of 4 lbs. of lead pigment to 1 pint of raw oil, which the first coating requires.

As some of the cornice is rather elaborately cast, thin with still more oil a part of this paint, and proceed to first coat the cornice only. In painting this portion, take every care not to break the delicate plaster work, using light and suitable-sized paint tools to coat both recessed and prominent parts.

Here, perhaps, it may be asked, Why not use the same paint and cover the wall as far down as you can reach at the same time as the cornice? The reply is that the plaster on the walls being well prepared and trowelled, it will be an advantage to use paint slightly thicker; and a full-sized paint-brush will be necessary to spread it over a large plain surface. It will be advisable also to strain the paint through a wire gauze paint strainer or piece of muslin before using it on the walls or wood-work.

As a rule, it is requisite to previously examine the walls and pick out the little blisters which have formed on the face of the plaster, and then to well wet the damaged place with water and make good with plaster; but this will not be necessary with the case in hand.

Now, with an old brush carefully work the paint through the strainer into another vessel, and slightly lower the plank or scaffold, so that it is possible to reach down half-way from cornice to skirting.

Re-commencing, first take a piece of partly-worn fine or middle 2 glass-paper, and lightly rub over the wall as far as can be reached; then with a dusting-brush and a downward movement remove any dust which has accumulated. With a full brush of colour now make a start from the right-hand extremity, and, working towards the left hand, cover about a yard in width at each shift. After taking a good dip of colour, gently draw the brush against the side of the paint-pot, and then carry the colour to the wall with an up-ended movement, and thus avoid waste in transit. Spread each of these brushfuls of paint about six inches apart with a long up and down movement, and when the patches extend about three or four feet in width, spread the paint evenly by repeated cross-brushing. Now it is roughly distributed, but is not sufficiently smooth, since the marks of the brush hairs show distinctly; the surface, therefore, has to be done over again with the brush, first with perpendicular and then with horizontal brushing, but no more paint, and each time with a lighter hand. Having finally drawn the tip of the brush down the work, starting each stroke from the top and working from right to left, it will be found that the marks of the brush are not noticeable, and that the paint is properly laid off. Move the paint-pot a little to the left and again commence laying on brushfuls, and spread and lay the paint off as before, until the upper half of one side of the wall is covered. Now descend and paint the lower half in a similar way, except that in the final laying off, finish with a light movement upward, from skirting to the join, so that all signs of this are removed.

Though all house-painters do not spread paint on this simple but regular system, yet for good work it cannot be excelled, and is, at least, preferable to any haphazard plan.

The painted walls must stand for at least a day, and meanwhile attention may be turned to the wood-work. Let us suppose by arrangement with the builder this has been left in the white or plain wood, with the exception of the sashes and window-frames, which have to be primed before being glazed, and so protected from the ill effects of wet weather before fixing. The sooner a coat of priming is put on new wood-work which is to be ultimately painted, the better; so touch over any knots in the wood with one or two coats of quick-drying patent knotting: this material prevents the resin exuding and discolouring the work. Then take some thin oil paint as used on the walls, and adding to it sufficient dry red lead to make it a full pink colour, prime the new wood-work. As with the wall, so with the wood-work—first lightly rub it down with glass-paper, and carefully dust the work. First paint the edge of the door and panel mouldings, then the panels themselves, working from the top downwards; proceed with the stiles between panels, the top, lock, and bottom cross rails, all brushed in the direction of the grain, and laying off the outer stiles last of all, which reach from top to bottom of the entire door. Careful spreading and systematic working are just as necessary for wood as for plaster, but whilst plaster is always laid off with up-and-down strokes, wood is always brushed in the direction of its grain.

The priming coat being now satisfactorily completed, proceed to the second coating.

Glance round the room before making up the paint, and get some idea of what is required. There is little evidence of oil paint on the white cornice plaster beyond the discoloration of its surface, so that the oil has all been absorbed into it. The walls, however, having been trowelled and finished, exhibit patches of the glossy paint on the surface; this shows that the absorption of paint is entirely stopped in those places, and probably nearly so all over. Under these circumstances, paint of the same kind, but with a little more lead in it, is required for the second coat upon the cornice, but for the walls the paint is made up considerably rounder or thicker, and instead of all oil, two parts of linseed to one of turps are used, with sufficient Venetian red in oil to give a decided pink cast; the mixture is then strained. This variation in tint not only makes it easy to see that no part is missed, but also has an agreeable influence of colour upon the succeeding coats.

The second coat being now spread upon cornice and walls, as before, return to the wood-work. Having lightly papered it down, dust it, and stop the nail-holes in the panel mouldings, etc., with putty made from white lead stiffened with best, or gilders', whiting. After stopping wood-work, it is advisable to let it stand a day, to allow the putty to harden on the surface. The second coat of paint can then be applied without affecting it; this should be of similar proportions to that last spread on walls. There are now two coats upon all the work, the absorption in cornice, wall, and wood-work being thereby effectually stopped.

Before considering the finishing colour of the painted work, attention must be turned to the ceiling. This is coated with clear-cole, to stop some of the suction of its porous surface; and having again become thoroughly dry, finish the cornice with three coats of white paint, and the flat, or bed, with a coat of faint pink distemper: a process fully described in a previous chapter.

It has been previously mentioned that in spreading a succession of coats of oil paint, upon plaster-work especially, it is not advisable to use two successive coats of *all oil* colour except for the purpose of stopping absorption; when that end is gained, it is necessary to mix the next coat with turpentine in a larger proportion than oil. To continue using successive layers of paint very oily causes each coat to harden in itself; but if sharp or turps paint be interposed between two coats of oil paint, the three coatings become firmly bound together. In *flatting* or dead-painting surfaces, this same system underlies the whole process. A last coat of oily paint, nearly identical in colour to the desired tint of flatting, is very carefully spread, and upon this *ground* the thin coating of purely turps colour is laid, generally the next day or next but one, before the ground becomes properly hard. This is the action that takes place providing the ground and flatting are properly prepared and manipulated: the oil of turpentine slightly opens the surface of the linseed oil ground beneath, so that this takes hold of the particles of pigment contained in the flatting, whilst the gradual evaporation of the turps leaves the surface without gloss, the pigment being held by the oil beneath, but uncovered upon its surface. Properly flatted wood-work and walls can be washed as safely as can oily paint, but the same knowledge of its nature is as necessary to successfully clean and preserve it as it is to prepare it. It is only when wrongly treated that flatting will not stand fair wear and tear.

Having determined to flat the cornice, it must be

previously grounded with oil paint, somewhat akin to the finishing flatting colour. The wall space may be left in a medium gloss of oil paint, so that the third coat must be of sharp colour and near the tint of the finishing paint. The cement skirting should now be first coated with the paint used on walls; then finish that and the wood-work with two more coats of good oil paint. This is with a view to present economy and the temporary nature of the job; permanent embellishment is to come later on.

Let us suppose here that the final colour of the walls has been decided upon, and that, in accordance with the remarks in the chapter on Colour, a dull soft-toned green has been chosen for the walls, relieved by the contrasts of complementary colours elsewhere.

To prepare the third coating and ground, the sharp wall colour is mixed in the proportions of twelve lead to one patent driers, with nearly three-fourths of turps to the remaining fourth of linseed oil. There is no need to measure exactly, but if the solids are beaten up in oil into thick batter consistency, it will require sufficient turps to thin it for use. Sufficient of the thick paint is put aside to suffice for the cornice, and before thinning the remainder for the walls, it is stained to warm green with Prussian blue, yellow ochre, and burnt umber, ground in oil. The exact shade is similar to, though much lighter than, sage green. To ensure a good solid wall when finished, this third coating paint is stained several shades *darker*, because a finishing tint will cover much better when laid upon a darker shade—a point to be remembered in oil painting. In mixing both this and the finishing wall paint, first stain the white to a medium blue, then add ochre to convert it into green, and lastly add the umber to soften and neutralise, or to warm the green mixture. Previous to spreading the " sharp "—that is, comparatively quick-drying paint—it is necessary to ground the cornice; but as it is intended to use some warm tints in contrast to the sage green walls, it is best to first mix colours for finishing the wood-work.

As some relief to the mass of wall colour, let the wood-work be painted in dark warm shades, such as Arabian brown and terra-cotta No. 3. Use the brown, which is the darker of the two, upon the entire door frame, the window frames, and the doors, with the exception of the panels and mouldings around same, and the deep bottom plinth of the skirting. Paint the panels of the wood-work, the window sashes, and top plinth of skirting with terra-cotta No. 3; and, with a view to brightening up the whole door, finish the panel mouldings and one member or division of the door frame with the soft sage-green wall colour. This method shows the advantage of deciding and making up the warm green dominant colour at the start, so that the remaining and contrasting colours may be compared with it, and a harmonious effect obtained. The colour for the woodwork is made from Venetian red and burnt umber chiefly, and Indian red, with the addition of a little ochre, lightened up with white for the panels.

The cornice may be treated in three main divisions. Paint that portion next the wall with a colour similar to the wood-work panels, but with the addition of a little more white and umber; the middle recessed division, or cove, paint with a slightly bluer grey and lighter tint of wall colour, made by adding to it a very little blue and white; and ground the third and top division of mouldings a lighter and more golden hue than the base part. These cornice paints are prepared from the thick white paint put aside for this purpose. A little of the wood-work and wall paints have been added for staining or colouring. They are now well strained and thinned with three parts oil and one of turps, and are spread according to the above arrangement. The wall is papered down, and any little indentations in the plaster are faced up with the same stopping as used for woodwork.

It is now third-coated with the soft sage-green colour, used darker than the desired finish, and with fully two-thirds of turps to one of oil. The third coat requires to be rather thicker than the two previous ones, and it must be well spread, laid off, and worked rather expeditiously, one flank or division of the wall at a time, to prevent the joints showing. The cement skirting is afterwards first-coated with the same colour spread very barely; as it is a comparatively non-absorbent surface, this sharp paint forms the best key for the finishing coat of dark red. Its present colour is no disadvantage, since the first coat of wood-work paint will effectually hide it.

Now the cornice is ready for flatting, and the walls for the fourth and last coat of oil paint. Break up lead and paste driers with former proportions of solids, but all turpentine, into batter consistency. Divide it into the quantity required for the three divisions of cornice, stain them a few degrees lighter than the respective oil-ground colours, using the blue, red, ochre, and umber pigments for staining, and then strain and thin with more turps, ready for use. The nature of the flatting process has been already explained; but the painter must now take each coat right along each flank: first, the light terra-cotta next to ceiling; then the green-grey recessed portion; and lastly, the bottom division of warm colour. If all three colours were brought along at once, the joints would invariably appear shiny, the effect of which, at intervals of every five or six feet, would be disagreeable, and would spoil the repose of the entire cornice.

Flatting requires to be very quickly done, and the brush must not touch the surface after the paint once commences to set, which it will do within a few minutes. When a large surface of wall is to be flatted, the paint must be spread entirely over it at once; so that, if single-handed, do not in this case attempt more than the cornice. If any small portions of a large place are missed in the flatting, the wall is spoiled, not so much by the colour of the part missed, but by the bright oily gloss of the ground. Use the flatting much thinner than the oil paint —almost as thin as milk—taking special care to coat all recessed as well as prominent portions, so that it all dries as dead and solid as the pink distempered ceiling.

All danger of splashing now being over, give the walls a final rub down with No. 1½ glass-paper, and finish them with the lighter tint of sage-green, prepared as before, but with two-thirds of oil to one of turps, which dries with a good medium gloss, and allows plenty of time to spread it over and lay it off.

Ceiling, cornice, and walls being now finished and dry, the skirting and wood-work alone remain. The paint for the latter is already made, but requires the addition of one of terebine to twelve or fourteen of paint, which is preferable to white driers in compounding this paint. Thin sufficient of this with two parts of turps to one of oil; carefully rub down and face up the work, taking special care not to rub the previous coat off the sharp edges of the mouldings. Coat the wood on the system previously explained. The light panel paint is first spread, covering mouldings also this time; and then the brushes are well worked into the dark Arabian brown colour, and the remainder, including skirting, is painted. On the day following, the third coat will be quite hard, therefore finish it right off with the remainder of the thick mixed paint, but made to a working consistency with reversed quantities of liquids: namely, two-thirds linseed oil to one of turps, leaving the picking in of the panel mouldings with the sage-green wall colour until the next day.

Now look around, and gather up the lessons this room should have taught. There are different proportions of solids and liquids to compound oil, sharp, and flatting paints for walls and wood-work. A good notion has been obtained of the system of working or manipulating them, as well as the methods of thought required in deciding colours, from which latter it will have been gathered that successful colour results are the outcome of scientific arrangement—taste it is usually termed. The *necessity* for clean and careful work, dusting the work, and well straining the paint, and thereby saving much time and glass-paper, on new wood particularly, will be now thoroughly understood. As to the colour scheme of the billiard-room, perhaps, to those who have been used to black and amber drabs favoured by the builder, its present appearance may give the impression of being rather "loud." But when the billiard-table is fixed in the room, with its pure green cloth, the wall colour will assume a warmer and much more sombre tone, making a fine background for oil paintings in gilded frames; whilst the dark warm shades of the wood-work will correspond effectively with the mahogany framework of the table, and will suit equally well with any other articles of furniture usual to a billiard-room.

CHAPTER IX.

PAPERING A ROOM.

PAPER-HANGING, as a *distinct* trade, is but of recent date, originating within the last twenty or thirty years. In earlier days it was as often a carpenter's job as a painter's, and even now it is only in the largest trade centres that we find it followed as a separate branch of work. The wide range in materials and prices of paper-hangings—from the cheapest "pulps" at 2d. a piece to the "Japanese leathers" at 60s., now provided for all classes of houses and for all conditions of life—makes the subject of properly fixing paper hangings a wide one.

In papering a room, all the old paper should be first stripped off the walls. A painter's stopping-knife is very handy for this purpose. If it is found that this damages the wall too much, those parts that are thoroughly stuck to the plaster may be left; but it is much better to take it all off, being careful not to dig into the plaster with the knife. Carefully pull out all nails, etc. All loose or bad places should be cut out and made good with plaster of Paris or with a piece of brown paper pasted over them. When dry, give all the walls a coat of thin size (as when clear-coleing a ceiling). The sizing sometimes shows up loose pieces of paper not torn off. If this is so, tear them off, and touch the places with size again. It is very often a great deal of trouble to get varnished paper off walls, especially if the paper has been varnished *after* it is hung. If the paper is properly hung, and there is only one paper on the wall, it will hardly be necessary to take it off. If it is quite tight to the wall, and there is no fear of its stripping of its own accord, it will make a very good ground for the new paper. To prepare a varnished paper for re-papering, properly smooth down all joints and projecting pattern with glass-paper, then give the wall a good coat of strong size in which a little previously soaked whiting has been added. When thoroughly dry, rub this coat of size, or "sheepskin," down with glass-paper, and you will have a good surface on which to hang new paper. To re-paper, any good paper will do; but the sanitary papers—so-called washable—are the easiest to varnish. If it is, however, considered that the original varnished paper should come off, scratch it all over with an old fork, and hang wet sheets over the paper, keeping them wet and tight to the paper until the water has got behind the varnish; then strip the paper off with a wide chisel or stripping-knife. If this does not get the paper off, you must give it a coat of hot lime, taking care not to touch any painted work. After the paper is off, well wash the wall and surrounding wood-work with vinegar before sizing the wall for new paper.

The best way for a novice to cut the margins of the wall-paper is to unroll a piece of paper right along the length of the table or paste-board, letting the unrolled part fall on the floor at the further end. Then, sitting down, start cutting to the pattern, at the same time rolling the paper up with the left hand. When one edge is cut, turn the piece round and unroll it, again letting the unrolled part fall on the floor at the other end, as before, and trim the other edge, cutting right up to the pattern. Sharp paperhangers' scissors are best for this work, which must be done very carefully and true, so as to butt the edges together, and not lap them; therefore, they must be perfectly straight. The pattern is straight, so cut exactly to it in a series of cuts as long as the scissors will allow. The paper must now be re-rolled in the same way as it was originally. Bear in mind that the outside end of the piece is always the top of the paper Now proceed with the rest of the pieces in the same manner.

To make paste for paperhanging, put half a quartern of flour in a clean pail, and thoroughly mix it with clean cold water until it is of the consistency of thick cream, and then pour boiling water on it quickly out of a saucepan, mixing it all the time until it thickens. Then stand it by until it gets cold. Sometimes alum is put in it; about half an eggcupful of powdered alum would be an advantage, as it will prevent vermin breeding after the paper is hung. A small quantity of carbolic acid in the paste, besides repelling cockroaches and all other insects, will neutralise the disagreeable odour consequent upon the decomposition of the paste, which in newly-prepared walls, is sometimes very offensive. The cheapest and best form of carbolic acid is in crystals. These dissolve in warm water. If the paste is lumpy, it should be strained to remove the lumps, but these should not occur in properly made paste.

A piece of wall-paper is 20 in. wide, 12 yds. long, and contains 63 super. ft. or 7 sq. yds. Measure the length and the height of the walls in feet, and multiply them together; this gives the superficial feet of wall. Dividing the sum by nine gives the superficial yards, and then dividing by seven the number of pieces of wallpaper required. It is customary to allow one piece in ten for waste. Another way of measuring a room for papering, is to go round the room, marking off how many 20 in. there are round the walls, then reckon how many lengths can be got out of the 12 yds., allowing for waste; divide the number of 20 in. there are round the room by the number of lengths you can get out of the 12 yds., and this will give you the number of pieces required. A slip of wood exactly 20 in. long is handy for taking this special measurement.

The paperhanger needs a good table to work on—one at least 5 ft. 6 in. long, and if a table of sufficient length is not available, it will pay to buy two pine boards ½ in. thick by 11 in. wide, 6 ft. long. Lay them side by side on any support, and secure them together by two battens screwed on underneath. Cover one side of these boards with brown paper pasted on. These will now give a surface to work upon, and there will be no fear that a good table will be damaged. Light trestles are generally used for supporting the boards.

Now cut the paper into pieces of the lengths required. This is the difficult part, but attention to what follows will enable you to do this all right. First cut off a piece 2 in. longer than the height from the skirting to the ceiling, and pin it up in its place temporarily, so that there is 1 in. in excess at the top and 1 in. at the bottom. Now hold up by the side of it the uncut paper, and match the pattern; to do this, you must waste some paper; how much, depends on the pattern chosen the length of which is indicated by dots on the edge of the paper. Cut this next length off and tack it up, making the pattern match. Studying these two pieces will show what is required for the remainder.

The first piece can be taken down and laid on the paste-board, face upwards. Now take the next piece and make the patterns on the edges coincide, and carefully notice the position as they lie. Lay the second piece directly over the first; unroll the uncut paper, making the pattern match with the second on the edge opposite to that which matches the first. Cut off this, making the third piece, allowing enough; but not so much as will cut into the pattern for the other end of the next piece. Proceed in this manner until as many lengths have been cut as required. Now turn the whole pile face downwards, get all the edges even and about 3 in. away from the front edge of the board, letting both ends overhang the board equally.

An apron will be a protection against making the clothes dirty; one with a bib and a pocket in front is most convenient for all such jobs about the house. For a brush, a stiff hat-brush will serve, as it can be washed afterwards—but the brush made for the purpose will be better; a clean piece of rag about the size of an ordinary duster, and a wheel-castor, off a chair, fastened to a bradawl handle for rolling down the joints; these things, with a pair of scissors, should be in the pocket of the apron.

Paperhangers', or papering, brushes are as shown at Fig. 60; these are used for hanging new paper to walls, just in the way that a cloth is used by some persons. The shape of the back is somewhat similar to a spoke-

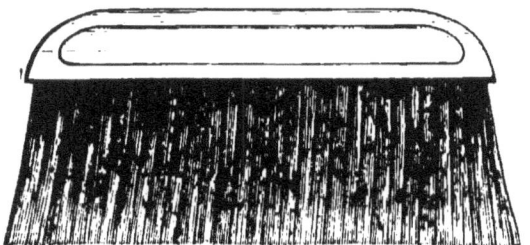

Fig. 60.—Paperhangers' Brush.

brush—long and thin, so that the hand can grasp it comfortably. Paperhangers use such a brush for the bulk of their work; but for "satin" goods and very

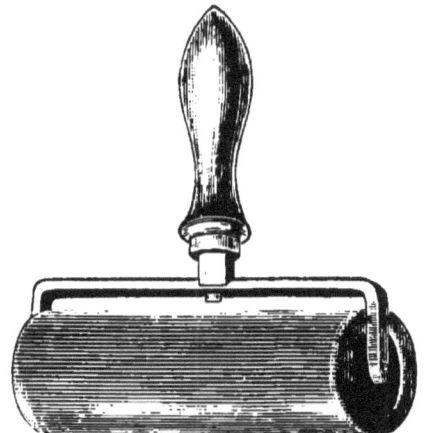

Fig. 61.—Paperhangers' Roller.

delicate papers the roller (Fig. 61) is substituted for the brush, and with this the paper is rolled into close contact with the wall. When newly purchased, it is usual to cover a roller neatly with a couple of thicknesses of flannel.

Now for hanging: work your paste-brush (Fig. 37, p. 66)

well into the paste, and clean it by scraping it on the edge of the pail. Keep the pail in one position, so that you scrape the brush against the same side, then when the brush is laid upon the top of the pail, the handle does not get covered with paste. Pull the top piece of paper towards you, so that the nearest edge comes about half an inch over the front edge of the board, and draw the paper to the left, till about half an inch of it overhangs the board on the right-hand end; that end which will be the bottom of the paper when hung. Paste this first piece, beginning at the bottom, and going the whole length of the board. You cannot paste the board, and any paste that goes on the next piece of paper at the back does no harm. Take hold of the bottom edge of the paper, and fold it back on itself, letting it lie without wrinkles lightly on the other pasted part, with the edges coinciding. Draw it from right to left along the board and paste the rest, being very careful not to let any paste get on the face side.

Conveying a length of pasted paper from the pasteboard to the wall is not so easy a process as it looks. One of the best methods that a professional worker will use for lengths of, say, about 8 ft. is as follows:—The lengths being cut to about the right size and properly arranged for clean pasting upon the pasteboard, the lower half is first pasted, and then folded over for about 18 in. or more of doubled length. The paper is moved along and the pasting completed; the upper edge is then folded over to the centre, and then the top edge turned right back. In conveying and fixing it, the top edge is taken hold of firmly, but carefully, by finger and thumb of each hand, and the fold is held by the other fingers. If working from a plank and scaffold, it is necessary, of course, to use one hand to get up to the work, in which case the top is folded as the bottom, and the length thrown over one arm. The difference between having the top edge in the fingers ready for matching and that of having to unfold the same has a marked effect in the speed of paperhanging.

See that the steps are convenient for mounting. Starting from one side of a window, carefully take the pasted piece of paper by the two top corners, a finger being on the pasted side and a thumb on the face side of the paper, raise the edge to the ceiling, and having previously plumbed the outside of the window-frame, see that the length hangs straight and upright with the window; gently press the top part of the paper against the wall sufficiently to hold its weight; draw the bottom away from the wall and undo the fold, letting the whole length hang free of the wall except the top six inches. See that it hangs plumb, and fix it there with a downward sweep of the brush in the centre, and then brush outwards both ways from the centre. The paper should now hang without a wrinkle. With the back of the scissors mark a line on the face of the paper along the angle where the wall joins the ceiling; draw the paper gently away and cut it along this line, brushing the paper back afterwards; then treat the bottom in the same manner. Now go over the whole with a clean cloth, dabbing it all over carefully, and roll the edges down with a wheel or castor. If the top or any other part needs a little adjusting, gently draw it away from the wall, and brush it back to its place.

Proceed with the next piece, taking care that the pattern matches and the joint butts exactly. Go round part of the room in this manner until you come to the door. There commence on the other side of the window and go round in the opposite direction, taking care to finish behind the door or in a dark corner. Frequently try the lengths with a plumb-bob, with the upper end of the line fastened round a bradawl, so that by lightly driving the bradawl into the plaster directly in the joint of the paper, you can at a glance see how you are getting on.

At internal angles, measure from the last piece hung up to the angle, and cut that width of paper on the paste-board, hang it, and then follow with the remainder. In all cases use such paper as will stand a lot of handling in the hanging, and from which any paste, etc., can be sponged off afterwards.

If a ceiling is to be papered, treat it in precisely the same manner as the walls, allowing, of course, for relative different positions. A small diaper pattern paper is perhaps most suitable for ceilings.

If a damp-proof paper is required, there are several kinds to be obtained, or the newly-hung paper might be varnished. To varnish paper, *great* care must be taken in the hanging. The paper should then be twice sized with clear size, put on just before it chills, being very careful to cover *every* bit with each coat of size; for wherever you miss in sizing, the varnish will turn that place dark. The same with the joints or any torn places—if the paper does not stick perfectly to the wall, the varnish will turn the places dark. When the size is quite dry, rub it over with a piece of brown paper, and then varnish with French oil-varnish if the paper is at all light coloured.

Varnishing the paper makes a decided improvement, but a paper fit for or worth varnishing cannot be obtained for much under 1s. per piece. Don't use good varnish on a common paper, if varnishing at all. Sanitary papers, from 1s. per piece upwards, are good value, and can be sponged, but not washed. Paper must be twice coated with patent size previous to varnishing. The size must be applied in liquid form; hence the print of the paper must be made so that it will not rub up.

Whilst the embellishments of the exteriors of our houses have increased, those of the interiors have declined, except where the expensive Japanese leather, or the elaborate Lincrusta Walton, or the modelled Tynecastle tapestry hold their sway.

Some of the fancy papers require special treatment. Embossed paper should be well soaked with paste, and allowed to remain a short time, to make it pliable. A roller with a china wheel—not a metal one—could be used for the edges with advantage, but be careful not to press too heavily. The ordinary roller should also be used, as well as the brush and cloth.

Japanese leather papers may be hung in the following manner:—

Having rigged up a paste-board or table, get a strip of zinc the length of paste-board; tack one end of it under the end edge, and flush with the edge of board next you. Draw and stretch it over top of the board to the other end, and tack it under in the same way. Now get a straight-edge of very hard wood, or, if possible, a steel straight-edge; a shoemaker's knife and a hone are indispensable tools. Roll out some paper, face upwards, at right-hand end of table. Sometimes this is rolled face or pattern side downwards. In this case, place a sheet beneath it, drag one end of it over top of table, and tie a piece of rag round a weight, and place that on the end, to keep it from curling back on you. The edge of the stuff is supposed to be lying along the middle of the zinc; place the straight-edge on the edge to come off, being careful not to cut straight down, but so that the edge of the knife inclines from you. This causes the edges of the paper when pressed together to form a close butt. When all the walls are rubbed down and sized, measure off each length on the wall, and where the joints come, run a brush full of flat same colour as ground of paper, for fear of shrinkage; if this is not attended to, and the paper happens to shrink as it dries, the gap looks very bad. As this kind of paper is heavily embossed, rub on plenty of paste, and if thick, let it soak; then fix the paper by patting it, and keep a small hammer and a few copper tacks handy.

The comparative value of a light-coloured wall-paper in a room has been calculated from systematic photometry to be as follows:—Supposing 100 candles give a certain light in a room covered with dead black cloth, 87 candles will give the same amount of light when dark brown paper is used. With blue paper, 72 are as effective; with fresh yellow paint, 60 candles; newly-dressed deal-boarded walls, 50 candles; but if papered or painted a pure white, 15 candles have as much lighting effect as the 100 when surrounded by black cloth-covered walls.

Wall-papers that contain arsenic are not always green in colour, although mostly so. To find if this injurious mineral is present, place a little of the suspected paper, torn into pieces, in a watch-glass and cover with liquor ammonia, letting this soak well in. Drop a small piece of lunar caustic upon the paper; the formation of a yellow precipitate shows the presence of arsenic. Many green papers contain no arsenic.

For the purpose of cleaning wall-papers the value of stale bread is very generally known, and its service more largely requisitioned than that of all other substances. It is well suited for the job, and deservedly in favour, but in many respects is not equal to the comparatively unknown dough process. This is cheaper, quicker, leaves no dust or crumbs about, and, with moderate care, will make an equally good job with a less expenditure of labour. The dough for this purpose is simply a mixture of coarse flour—the coarser the better—and water, mixed to a rather stiffer consistency than for a pudding. About 1 lb. or 1½ lbs. of flour will be sufficient to clean the walls of one good-sized room, even though the paper be very dirty. The loose dust on the walls should first be removed by a soft broom or brush, and then the lump of dough passed lightly over the paper, when it will be seen to remove the dirt in its path as effectively as an indiarubber squeegee removes liquid mud from an asphalte road. The dough in use softens as it works, and in consequence it will be found desirable to have some flour in a bowl to roll it in occasionally.

If not intended to wash the ceiling, it may with advantage be treated the same as the walls, though if thus done, it will not, of course, have the brilliant whiteness of a fresh-distempered ceiling. By this means it is quite possible to thoroughly clean the walls and ceiling of a fair-sized room in less than an hour. Even though the walls and ceiling may be very smoky and dirty before cleaning, and the walls show by very pronounced patches the parts that have been covered by pictures, furniture, etc., when finished they will present an evenly clean appearance, suggestive of new paper; the ceiling also will look clean and presentable, though previously blackened by smoke. For simplicity, ease, cheapness, and the facility with which this work can be done by anyone without previous experience, the dough method of cleaning commends itself.

If the stains on the paper to be cleaned are the result of moisture or dampness, it will be a waste of time and trouble to clean them. The remedy is to use a waterproof paper, or to treat the walls in some way.

CHAPTER X

SIMPLE EMBELLISHMENT OF WALLS AND CEILINGS.

Some of the methods by which the embellishment of walls and ceilings can be achieved are extremely simple, and their effectiveness when finished is far out of proportion to the smallness of the time, the labour, and the

Fig. 62.—Four Designs for Ashlar Work Dado.

cost involved. Some of these methods it is intended briefly to indicate in this chapter, and the reader who has attentively perused the previous pages will find no difficulty in following out the directions which follow.

Fig. 62 shows a simple treatment in ashlar work suited for ornamenting a dado. There are four distinct patterns shown in the illustration; they are distinguished by numbers, and, of course, one pattern only would be adopted for one dado.

A ground colour of plain Bath stone with lines of dark red would be an effective scheme. The lines are made with a straight-edge and lining fitch, in the way described on a previous page.

Fig. 63 represents a simple plaster cornice, embellished with a frieze border stencilled below it. Fig. 64 shows the pattern to be stencilled just above the skirting-board. Ornaments of these designs are of the simplest kind, and by their regular repetition of simple forms are suggestive of Greek decoration. Such an

Fig. 63.—Coloured Plaster Cornice, with Stencilled Frieze.

arrangement of base and frieze borders is suitable for bedrooms and parlours; a deeper frieze is more ornamental if skill and other circumstances permit.

Supposing a cool but cheerful room, with a greeny-blue tint as the dominant colour-sensation. The ceiling is tinted ivory or cream white, preferably a tint of raw sienna, as chromes are too bright. This will "throw up" the colour of walls by force of colour contrast. The wall colour made from white stained with blue, a little green, and a little umber is put on the top section of cornice, B. The cornice cove, A, is painted a dull "old gold," and a darker shade of wall colour forms its base, C. These three colours are advised for the wood-work of the room; panels to be coloured same as wall mouldings, "old gold"; and the stiles and rails, and other woodwork, a much deeper tone of wall colour.

J

It is suggested the width between the thick inner lines of the frieze be 6 in., and base borders 8 in. But this width can be increased or diminished at pleasure. The ornament and lines may be either in a darker tone of the wall colour or in old gold. A more striking contrast between pattern and ground is made with the ornament of a nut-brown colour; this colour may be used for lines, and deep grey or old gold for the stencils.

The deep frieze (Fig. 65) and base border (Fig. 66)

Fig 64.—Grecian Style Pattern for Stencil.

shown on page 147, may well be adapted to a dining- or living-room, or even to the walls of a library or study.

This frieze is essentially a decorative one, and it is not wise to apply this design to the lower part of a wall which has a great amount of wear. Assuming a room the lower part of which gets much hard wear: Mark out and paint a dark dado or base division, from 24 in. to 30 in. in height from top of skirting. Above this, and on the light ground of filling space, stencil the base border with the dado colour, using for the margin lines a still darker shade, or black.

A frieze as well as a dado is an acceptable feature in dining-rooms where the height of walls is not less than 11 ft. or 12 ft. The design given in Fig. 65 may, however, be used in rooms of even less height, because the *depth* of the frieze division can be lessened to any extent.

The lower stencil in Fig. 65 may be done in a deep brown-red; but if done in two colours, use the brown-red for the base-line and battlement lines and boss, and use a light, greeny, old gold for the "lily" ornament. The fine filling line may also be done in the frieze blue

Fig. 65.—Design for Stencil Frieze.

Fig. 66.—Design for Base Border.

colour when the wall filling used is sufficiently light to show up a blue.

Other tints suggested for this design (Fig. 65) are a faint blue tint for the ceiling, corresponding to the frieze blue. The simple floral ornament (A), stencilled on the grey ceiling with the brown stencil colour and with a line next cornice, will greatly relieve the bareness of a

148 *House Decoration.*

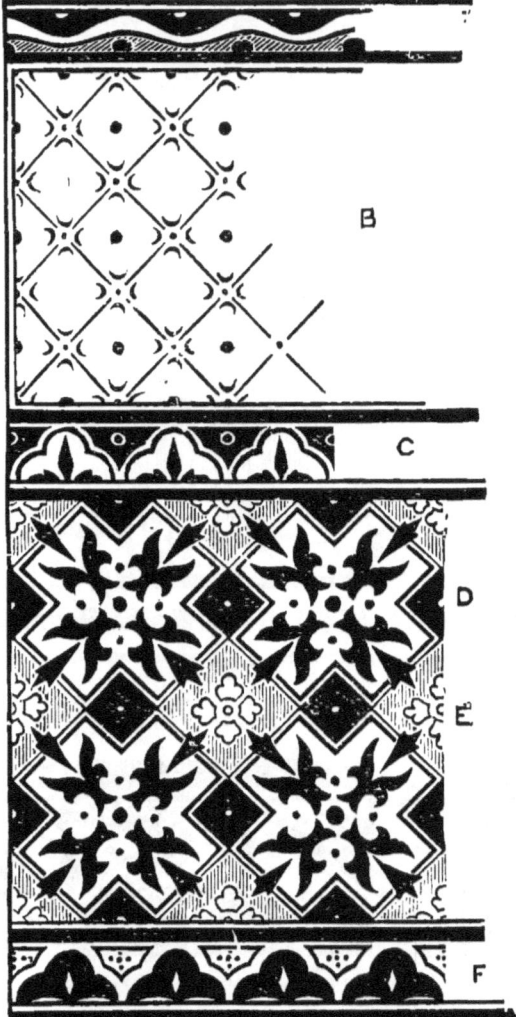

Fig. 67.—Stencil Designs for entire Wall.

ceiling. The woodwork may be painted plain dark reds, with blue moulding, or dark gobelin-blue stiles, buff panels, and red-brown mouldings.

The next set of designs (Fig. 67) shows a design for a "diaper" dado in which D E may be taken to represent a height of 24 in., which the borders, top (c) and bottom (F), each 6 in. in width, make a total height of three feet, exclusive of skirting. If this be too high, the bottom

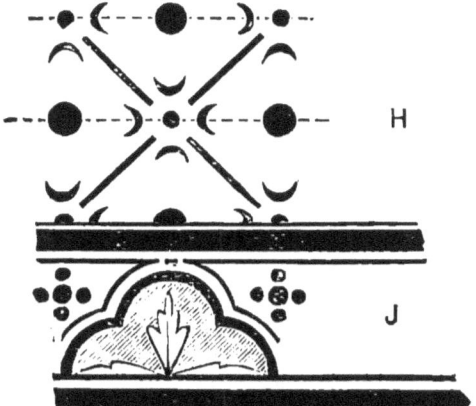

Fig. 68.—Design for Filling enlarged.

border may be omitted, a dark line alone terminating the design. Figs. 68 and 69 show portions of the dado,

Fig. 69.—Design for Dado enlarged.

border, and filling designs enlarged to twice the previous proportions. These will enable the reader to set out the work, and also to see where the "ties" are arranged.

A very handsome effect can be obtained with the design in two colours upon the dado ground. Two stencils, one for each colour, will be required for this treatment.

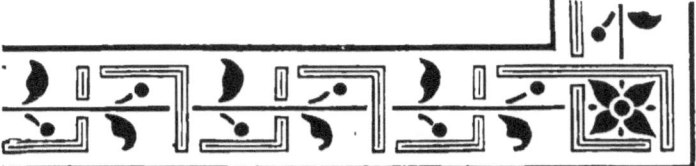

Fig. 70.—Border Ornament for Ceiling.

The wall is set out in 12 in. squares, and the stencil corresponds; first stencil one colour right through, when that is dry, stencil the other. Carefully set out, and carefully drawn and cut, this design can be executed

Fig. 71.—Deep Frieze Ornament.

more speedily than at first glance the reader may suppose. The filling stencil is of so simple a nature, it needs no analysing.

Room decoration in the Italian style shown by Figs. 70, 71, and 72, may seem a formidable task. These stencils have been arranged with a particular aim to their use for a drawing-room or best parlour, and as giving a sensation of more decided elegance and delicacy of environment than does either of the previous designs.

We have a deep frieze (Fig. 71), a base, scroll-pattern border (Fig. 72), and an ornament for the ceiling (Fig. 70). It will be seen that the frieze design will require much more care in enlarging than the one shown by Fig. 65, and also that it cannot be extended in the same manner as the latter. Some alteration in depth may be

Fig. 72.—Base Border Ornament.

effected with the dark border-band on top. This may be omitted, or, to gain width, may be repeated as a base-band to the frieze.

It will be noticed that two ground colours are suggested in the base-border (Fig. 72). On this feature much of the charm of the effect will depend, and it well repays the trouble of first painting in the upper half with a darker or contrasting colour.

The chief danger, and one that must be avoided at all cost of colour prettiness, lies in the colours and tones not being balanced—that is to say, we must keep the design equally distinct and plain throughout, and not "dying away into the wall" in some portions. The blending of stencil ornament is scarcely a task for the novice, and perhaps the best results will be met with when the colour-charm is present in the contrasting *masses of colour*, and the designs kept full in contrast and pleasing by reason of their form and arrangement of line and curve.

A deep "Gobelin" or "greenish" blue may be used for stencilling the frieze design, or a marone brown. The base scroll (Fig. 72) should be stencilled with similar colour, upon grounds of medium gobelin blue (upper) and wall colour (lower portion). If the frieze design is done in blue, use marone brown for the margin

Fig. 73.—Design for Border.

Fig. 74.—Design for Border.

band, which is, of course, put in with a small separate stencil. The cornice will be in old gold, creams, etc., *in tone* with wall filling; the ceiling grey, and the ceiling stencil in blue and marone brown upon a margin having old gold ground. The woodwork of room should be nut-brown and fawns, with a little gilding.

The four figures which follow show designs of the Adams' type—named so after the introducers of this style of decoration—which consists chiefly of repetitions of simple forms delineated in graceful lines.

Fig. 73 is a border pattern with a series of plain horizontal lines. Fig. 74 is another design, which may

EMBELLISHMENT OF WALLS AND CEILINGS. 153

Fig. 75.—Deep Frieze Decoration.

Fig. 76.—Dado in Borders and Panels.

be repeated as often as necessary to go round a room. Fig. 75 is a pattern that repeats itself in 36 inches. Fig. 76 is a dado, 36 in. high, with panels alternating in widths of 9 in. and 18 in.

The embellishment of ceilings offers great scope for the decorator. Fig. 77 shows a design for stencilling in

Fig. 77.—Corner of Ceiling Stencilled in Colours.

colours, the corner being so arranged that four stencils will join and make a centre ornament.

The way to draw this stencil is shown on p. 155. The point, A, is taken as centre, and arcs are drawn at intervals of 6 in. The corner angle is divided into two, and then one half is divided into four. By these means small drawings can be enlarged to any extent.

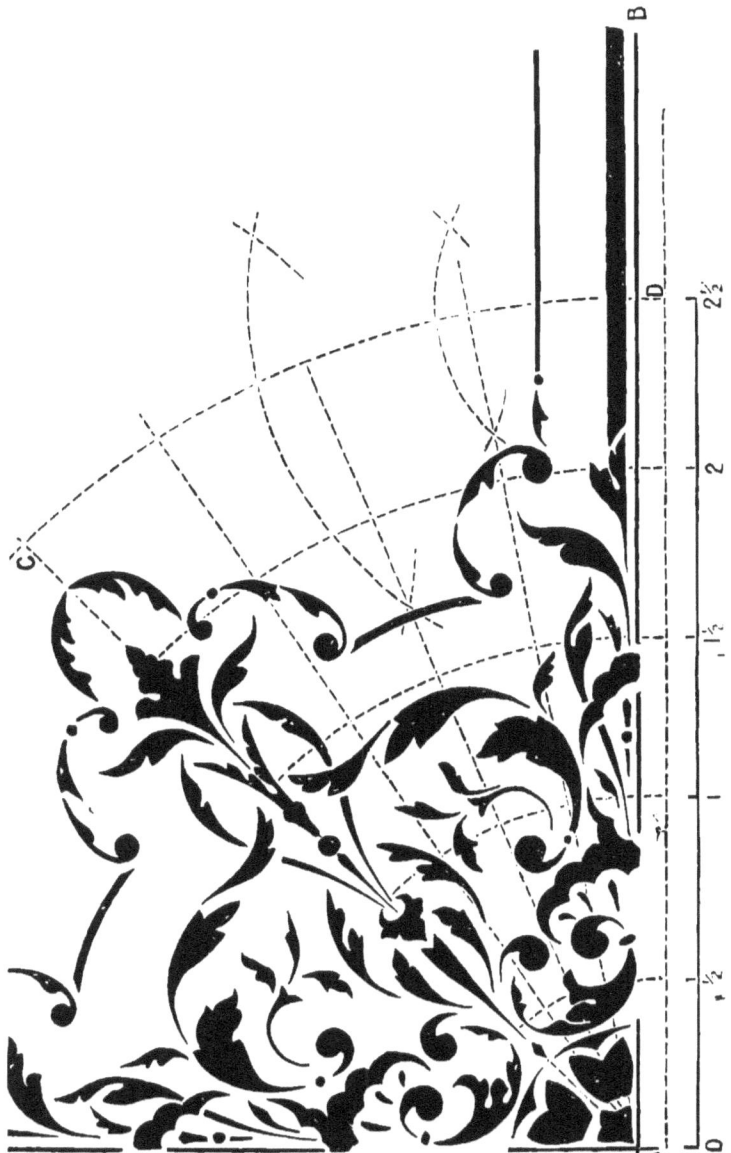

Fig. 78.—How to draw a Stencil.

Fig. 79 shows one quarter of a ceiling 14 ft. square without plaster central ornament. The illustration is

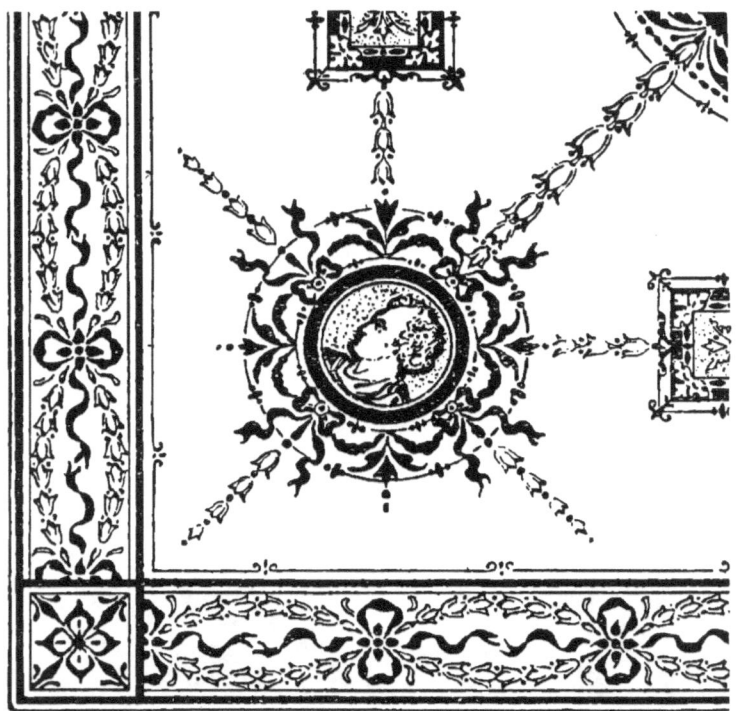

Fig. 79.—Design for Ceiling Embellishment.

drawn to a scale of ½ inch to a foot, and the reader can prepare from it all necessary drawings to working size.

INDEX.

A

Adams' Designs, 152
Adulteration of Brushes, 60
—— —— Pigments, 45
—— —— Turpentine, 53
—— —— White Lead, 58
Alum, Use of, in Distemper, 98
Antwerp Blue, 29
Apron, Paper-hanger's, 136
Arsenic in Wall-papers, 142

B

Balcony, Portable, for Painting Windows, 12, 13
Bastard Flat, 162
Bedroom Decoration, 18
——, Suitability of Distemper for, 91
Beeswax, Use of, in Distempering, 99
Berlin Black, 54
Bidwell, Professor, on Colour, 12
Billiard Room Painting and Decorating, 25, 123-132
Binders for Distemper, 93, 94
Black Chalk, 29
——, Japan, 54
—— Lead, 29
—— Paint, 29
—— Pigments, 28, 29
Blue Black, 28
—— Pigments, 29-32
—— Verditer, 32
Borders for Walls and Ceilings, 150-152
Bronze Green, 33
—— Yellow, 90
Brown Pigments, 32
Bristles for Making Painters' Brushes, 59
Brush, Stippling, 122
Brushes for Distempering, 65, 66
—— —— Dusting, 64
——, Painters', 59, 70
——, ——, Preserving, 69
——, ——, Tying, 68, 69
——, Paperhangers', 137
—— for Stencilling, 64
——, Varnish, Preserving, 70
—— for Washing, 65
Burnt Sienna, 38

C

Ceiling, Decorating, 145-147, 154
——, Distempering, in Pink, 108-110
——, Papering, 110
——, Stains on, 105
——, Stopping Cracks in, 105
——, Whitewashing, 103-105
Cement Wall Skirting, Painting, 121
Charlton White, 43
Chemical and Mechanical Action, Distinction between, 27
—— Nature of Pigments, Necessity for a Knowledge of, 76
Chromes, Medium, 33
——, Pale, 32
——, Yellow and Orange, 32
Cinnabar, 37
Cleaning a Room, 110
Cleanliness, Necessity for, 91, 123
Clear-cole, 94, 96, 98
Cobalt Blue, 29
Colour, Combinations of, 24
——, Constants of, 11
——, Definition of, 9
—— Distinguished from Pigment, 9
—— Harmony, 16
——, Lord Rayleigh on, 12
——, Professor Bidwell on, 12
——, Reducible to Formulæ, 13
—— Testing, 44
——, The Relationship of, to form, 16, 17
Colours, Common, 76
——, Complementaries of, 14, 15
——, Contrasts of, 16
——, General Remarks on, 75, 76
——, Impressions produced by, 15
——, Names of, 75
——, Oil, 10, 81-90
—— of Opaque Objects, 12
——, Primary, 13, 14
——, Secondary, 14
——, Superior, 76
——, Tertiary, 14
Complementary Colours, 14, 15
Constants of Colour, 11
Contrast in Colour, 16
Cornices, Decorating, 112, 145
——, Distempering, 107
——, Painting, 129, 130
——, The Use of, 23
——, Tinting, 18-24

D

Dadoes, 146, 149, 153
Damp Walls, 121
Damp-proof Wall-paper, 140
Decoration, Italian Style of, 150
Dining-room Decoration, 20, 22
Distemper, Definition of, 11
——, Mixing Tints of, 101
—— Tool, Use of, 108
——, Washing off, 104
Distempering, 91-102, 108-110
——, Brushes for, 65, 66
——, Pigments used in, 102
Dough for Cleaning Walls, 142
Drawing-room Decoration, 21, 22
Driers, 55-57

E

Earth Blacks, 29
Egg-shell Gloss, 97
Embellishments of Interiors of Houses, 140
—— —— Walls and Ceilings, 144-156
Emerald Green, 33
English Paint Tools, 61
Experience, Necessity of, to the Decorator, 26

F

Facia-writing, 9
Filling up Cracks and Nail-holes, 99
Fitches, 63
Flake White, 44
Flatting, 119, 121, 127, 130
——, Brushes for, 67
Fluorescence of Paraffin, 57
Formulæ for describing Colour, 13
French Grey Paint, To make, 80
—— Round Tool, 63
Friezes, 145-147, 153

G

Gamboge, 33
German Paint Tools, 61
Gilders' Fat Oil, 48
Glue for Distemper Purposes, 94
—— Powder, 96
Green Pigments, 33, 45
—— really a Primary Colour, 12

H

Halls and Staircases, Decoration of, 22
Harmony of Colours, 16, 25
House-Painter: his Work described, 9
Hue, 11

I

Indian Reds, 36
Indigo Blue, 30

Invisible Green, 33
Italian Style of Decoration, 150
Ivory Black, 28

J

Japan, 54, 55
Japanese Leather Papers, Hanging, 141
Jones, Owen, on Colour as applied to Form, 16
——, ——, on Colour Combinations, 24

K

Kalsomining, 94, 99
Knives, Chisel, 71, 72
——, Glaziers', 72
——, Painters', 71, 72
——, Stopping, 71
Knotting, 55, 115, 116

L

Lake Colours, 34
——, Yellow, 90
Lamp Black, 28
Library, Decoration of, 22
Lime, Blue, 31
Limers, 67
Luminosity, 11

M

Madder Lake, 34
Mechanical and Chemical Action, Distinction between, 27
Mixing Paints, 74-90

N

Names of Colours, 75
—— —— Pigments, 75
Nottingham White, 44

O

Ochres, 34, 36
Oil, Boiled, 48
—— Colour, 9
—— Colours, How to Mix, 74-90. (The various oil colours are alphabetically arranged in the text, and are therefore not separately indexed.)
——, Gilders' Fat, 48
—— of Turpentine, 9, 49
Olive Green, 33

P

Paddle Brush, 67
Paint, Cleaning, 115
——, To Distinguish Zinc from Lead, 46
——, Removing, 114, 115
——, The Uses of, 9

Painting, The Criterion of Good Workmanship in, 119
—— Plaster Surface, 120
—— a Room, 114-132
Paints, Bases of, 75
——, Oil, Mixing, 74-90
Paper, Stripping, off Walls, 133
Paper-hanging, 133
Paper Hangings, Material for, 133
Papering Ceilings, 140
—— a Room, 133-143
Papers (see Wall Papers.)
Paris Green, 33
Paste for Paper-hanging, 134
Patches, Brown, on Painted Surface, 120
Plaster Surface, Oil Painting, 120
Photometry, 141
Pigments, Adulterants of, 45
—— Distinguished from Colour, 9
——, The Manufacture of, 27
—— that must not be Mixed, 76
—— , Names of, 75
——, Qualities of Good, 27
—— for Staining Whiting, 102
Preserving Paint Brushes, 69, 70
—— Varnish Brushes, 70
Primary Colours, 14
Priming, 116
Prussian Blue, 30
Purity of Tints, how Obtained, 100
Purple Brown, 35

R

Raw Sienna, 38
Rayleigh, Lord, on Colours, 12
Red Lead, 35, 55
—— Ochres, 36
—— Pigments, 35-37
Roller, Paperhangers', 137
Room, Cleaning, 110
——, Decoration, 145-156
——, Measuring, for Wall-paper, 135
——, Painting, 118, 119
Royal Blue, 31
Ruskin, Mr., on Colour as applied to Form, 16

S

Sash Tools, 61, 62
Scaffold-board for Whitewashing, 104
Scales of Tones, 12
Secondary Colours, 14
—— ——, Compounding, 77
Siennas, Raw and Burnt, 38, 76
Sieve for Straining Paints, 70, 71
Silver White, 44
Sitting-room Decoration, 19
Size, 94, 96
——, Japanners' Gold, 55
—— Powder, 96
Spirit of Turpentine, 9

Stains, Removing, from Ceiling, 105
——, Varnish, 54
Staircases, Decoration of, 22
Stencil Brushes, 64
——, How to Draw a, 154
Stencilling, 145, 151, 152, 154
Stipplers, 67
Stippling Brush, 122
Stopping, 117
Straight-edge, 64
Straining Paints, 70, 71
Study, Decoration of, 22
Sublimation, 27
Suction of Cornice and Walls, To Stop, 123
Surface, Relation of, to Covering Material, 79, 98

T

Table for Paperhanger, 135
Tempera, 11
—— Painting, 91-102, 108-110
Terebine, 56, 57
Terms, Definitions of, 11
Terra di Sienna, 38
Terra Vert, 38
Tertiary Colours, 14, 44, 45
—— ——, Compounding, 77
Testing Brushes, 60
—— Oxide Paints, 45
—— Turpentine, 49, 58
—— White Lead, 46
Tone, 11
Tones, To Prepare a Series of, 12
Tools, English Paint, 61
——, German Paint, 61
——, Painters', 64-73
——, Paperhangers', 136, 137
Turkey Red, 37
Turpentine, Adulterants of, 58
——, Oil of, 9, 49
——, Spirit of, 9
——, Testing, 49, 58
Tying Paint Brushes, 68, 69

U

Ultramarine Blue, 31
—— Factitious, 32
Umbers, Raw and Burnt, 39, 76

V

Vandyke Brown, 32
Varnish, 10, 50-54
——, Bath, 54
——, Cheap Oak, 52
——, Church Oak, 52
——, Copal, 51, 52
——, Hard-Drying, 52
——, Maple, 53
——, Mastic, 51
——, Oil, 51
——, Removing, from Woodwork, 115

Varnish Stains, 54
—— for Wall Papers, 53
——, White Hard, 53
Varnishing, 49
——, Brushes for, 63
——, Time of Year for, 122
—— Wall Papers, 140
Vegetable Black, 29
Vehicles, 9, 54
Venetian Red, 37
Verdigris, 34
Vermilion, 37
——, The Manufacture of, 27

W

Wall-paper, 133
——, Arsenic in, 142
——, Cleaning, 142
——, Comparative Value of Light-coloured, 141
——, Cutting, into Lengths, 136
——, —— Margins of, 134
——, Damp-proof, 140
——, Fancy, 140
——, Hanging, 133, 139
——, Sanitary, 134
——, Size of, 135
——, Varnishing, 140
Walls and Ceilings, Embellishment of, 144–156
——, Dusting 124
——, Glass-papering, 124
——, Painting, 122, 125, 126, 130

Walls, Papering, 133-143
——, Preparing for, Papering, 133, 134
——, Sizing, 134
——, Washing, 134
Washing Flatted Wood-work and Walls, 127
White, Effect of Mixing, with Colours, 13
—— Lead, 39–42, 46, 75, 93
—— ——, Adulterants of, 46
—— ——, Antidotes for, 40
—— ——, Effect of, on Colour, 40
—— ——, Manufacture of, 41
—— ——, Substitutes for, 42
—— ——, Testing, 46
Whiting, 39, 93, 94
Whitewash, Preparing, 97, 106
Whitewashing, 97, 103–108
——, Causes of Unsuccessful, 108
Wine Colour, 89
Woodwork, Old, Painting and Distempering, 120
——, Painting, 125, 126, 129, 131

Y

Yellow Bronze, 90
—— Lake, 90
—— Pigments, 32–34
—— not a Primary Colour, 13

Z

Zinc White, 43, 44, 75

www.ingramcontent.com/pod-product-compliance
Lightning Source LLC
Chambersburg PA
CBHW030435190426
43202CB00036B/929